JORDEN BEACON

Uncovering Greek Knowledge

Understanding the Complete Greek Culture

Contents

I   Foundations of Greek Civilization

1   Introduction to the Land and Its People   3
History of Greece   3
Greek Mentality   7
Greek Character   10
Greek Hospitality   16
Greek Language   19
Religion of Greece   23
Greek Clothing   26
2   Processes of Democratization in Ancient Greece   27
The Aristocracy of Athens: Appearance and Role   27
Mechanism of political domination   29
The role of the people   31
Informal Power: The Beginning of the Struggle   32
3   The Gods and Mythology   36
Gods of Ancient Greece (Olympus)   37
Other gods of Olympus   41
Apollo - god of the arts, poetry, and healing   41
Ares - god of war   42
Artemis – goddess of the hunt   42
Athena – goddess of wisdom and war   42
Aphrodite – goddess of love and beauty   43
Nemesis - goddess of retribution   43

Helios - the sun god   44

Hemera - goddess of the day   44

Hera - goddess of family ties   45

Hermes - god of trade, messenger of Zeus   45

Hestia - goddess of the hearth   46

Hephaestus - god of blacksmithing (fire)   46

Hymen - god of marriage   47

Hypnos - god of sleep   48

4 Literature and Philosophy   49

Ancient Greek science. Philosophy   49

Ancient Greek science. Philosophy   53

Literature   55

Architecture   56

II   Pillars of Greek Thought and Culture

5 Philosophy and the Pursuit of Wisdom   61

Presocratic Thinkers and Questions about the Universe   62

Socrates, Plato, and the Development of Idealism   66

Hellenistic Philosophy and its Impact on Later Civilizations   73

6 Science and Mathematics: Seeking Knowledge
   of the World   77

Mathematics Knowledge   77

Medical Knowledge and Hippocrates' Contributions   84

7 Education and Rhetoric   89

Education System In Ancient Greece   89

Rhetoric In Ancient Greece   91

8 Theatre and Performance   98

History of the theater   98

Theatrical Action in Ancient Greece   100

Acting and costumes   100

Architecture of Ancient Greek Theater   102

III   Legacy and Influence

9 Greek Culture in the Modern World   107
Democracy   107
Science   109
Philosophy   110
Art   111
Architecture   112
Olympic Games   112
10 Rediscovering Greek Knowledge   114
Meeting the Arab World with Ancient Greek Knowledge   115
11 Alexander the Great and the Spread of Hellenistic Culture   118
Hellenistic era in the Middle East   119

I

Foundations of Greek Civilization

1

Introduction to the Land and Its People

Greek culture goes back thousands of years and is deservedly considered one of the most original and ancient in the world! Greece, Great Hellas, is a country that gave the world the Olympic Games and philosophy, democracy, and classical architecture, one of the most widespread writing systems and a rich literature that spread its influence throughout Europe and half of Asia. Ancient Greece truly made the greatest contribution to the culture and development of human society, and it cannot be underestimated.

History of Greece

The civilization of Ancient Greece played an important role in the development of mankind. Science, philosophy, art, politics, and many languages originate in Ancient Greece. In mathematics textbooks, from century to century, almost the same definitions that Euclid gave in his time were rewritten, and artists and poets rewrote the images of Hercules, Zeus, Apollo, Achilles, Pericles, Homer, and Alexander the Great. For everything that modern people are fighting for now, for freedom, truth, and equality, the Greeks also fought many thousands of years ago. And by the way, we can safely say that they achieved their goal, no matter what it cost them. If you want to better understand the modern world, the development of which has been based on all eras, you need to become as close as possible to the history of Ancient Greece.

We will begin our story with antiquity. So, the territory of Greece has been inhabited since ancient times, and there is no room for surprise here. After all, thanks to the favorable geographical location, favorable maritime climate, and generous nature, everything was possible. But, unfortunately, many Greeks emigrated to nearby and distant lands in search of food, Ancient culture, art, and philosophy began in the 5th-4th centuries BC. The era was called the Golden Age of Pericles.

The ancient Greeks were not like modern colonialists. They merged with them, all thanks to their knowledge and their developed culture. Ancient Hellas blossomed and flourished beyond the borders of the Balkan Peninsula, far from the islands of the Aegean Sea. This kind of settlement developed in its way, and as a result, today thousands of people on earth recognize themselves as real Greeks, even those who cannot even speak a single word of Greek. Descendants of the Greeks live in Afghanistan, Uzbekistan, India, Africa, and Latin America.

We can safely say that this unusual country is the cradle of a series of great civilizations: the Minoan civilization settled on the island of Crete and was destroyed by a volcano, the Mycenaean civilization centered in Tiryns, and the civilization of Troy, which was not a figment of the imagination of the elder Homer, also existed as a city-state, with its own culture, the Macedonian kingdom.

During its existence, Greece managed to survive a large number of conquerors: these were the Romans, the Turks, the Crusaders, and Philip II of Macedon, the father of Alexander the Great. The centuries-old Turkish yoke left the greatest residue in the creation of modern Greeks. However, it was the Crusaders who became the impetus for the accession of the Turks on the soil of Greece, who, on their way to liberating the Holy Sepulcher from the Muslim people, managed to conquer, for an unknown reason, the Orthodox Christian capital of Constantinople. This event dates back to 1024. They conquered Greek cities and weakened the Byzantine Empire so much that they could not withstand the onslaught of the troops of Mehmet II (1453) and finally disappeared under Turkish rule. It can be added that in 2001, Pope John Paul II visited Greece and publicly asked for forgiveness from all Orthodox Christians for the events that occurred five hundred years ago.

Middle Ages and Modern Times. The Greeks call the period of Ottoman rule "400 Turkish years". The National Liberation Revolution put an end to this difficult period, which began in 1812. Not the plan for the Revolution was developed by the secret organization of Greece "Filiki Eteria", created in Odessa. There is one more fact: in 1827, the first ruler of free Greece was the former Russian Foreign Minister and close associate of Tsar Alexander I - the Liberator - Ioannis Kapodistrias. In 1831, he was treacherously killed for his pro-Russian morals. During this period, the free country of Greece changed two capitals - the island of Aegina and the city of Nafplio.

Greece returned in 1833-1862 to a monarchy led by Otto, a Bavarian prince. Even though he was famous among the Greek people, the monk managed to make his contribution to the development of the country. He moved the capital to Athens and brought the ancient city, which at one time resembled an ordinary village, into a proper European state.

The post of King Otto from 1863 to 1913 was occupied by the European nobleman Danish Prince Wilhelm Glicksburg. George the First reigned on the throne of Greece along with his wife Olga Konstantinovna, Grand Duchess of the House of Romanov. For Greece, the nineteenth century ended with defeat in the war with the Turks, which led to the payment of large indemnities, the bankruptcy of the country, and the borrowing of huge funds from the IEC (International Economic Commission).

Twentieth century. Today, For Greece, the twentieth century was notable for its bankruptcy and complete economic recovery, a series of military victories and defeats. The country, it may be noted, liberated northern Greece from the Turkish yoke in 1913. But, unfortunately, the people of Greece were not able to fully enjoy the victory: in 1915, the Young Turks of Kemal Ataturk massacred all Armenians, in 1919 they massacred three hundred thousand Pontic Greeks, in 1922 the Greeks were exterminated once again by Turkish troops. Subsequently, almost millions of residents left their homes and lands to save their lives.

Following the Asia Minor catastrophe, an exchange of populations began: the Turks, who had lived in the lands of Greece for centuries, were evicted to Turkey, and the Greek population in Turkey to Greece. The country, almost until the middle of the 20th century, was under the yoke of dictators. One of the dictators, in response to a request issued by the Italian fascist state in 1936, gave a laconic, tough, and daring answer with one word "OHI", that is, "NO". The Greek people remembered this word for a long time. Today, the twenty-eighth of October is considered a holiday among the Greeks and is one of the two main public holidays.

Some time later. Greece, like Europe, was drawn into the Second World War, where it again reconciled the claims of the Italian people to the lands of Greece. But this time, not a single word was spoken, a weapon was taken into hand. Greece, unfortunately, was unable to resist the German onslaught, and the enemy managed to occupy the country. The Greeks, as a courageous and courageous people, held out to the last, and even being occupied by German troops, they did not give up even a share of their territory to Bulgaria, an ally of Germany, which encroached on their lands.

Greek Mentality

The Greeks, according to an international study, are the most insecure nation in the world. Hiding behind the facade of external dignity, they try to hide their doubts, and their insecurities by any means. They are afraid that they will be considered not serious enough, and the more shortcomings they find in themselves, the more pompous and serious they try to seem.

The Greeks are a huge tangle of contradictions. They are happy to criticize other Greeks for minor offenses, but if someone from another nation even slightly doubts that the Greeks are the salt of the earth, then this stranger will not be happy! The Greeks would attack him, blaming him for all the sins his country had committed against Greece since the dawn of civilization, and maybe even earlier. Modern Greeks, although they cannot boast of even a hundredth of the achievements of their ancestors, were nevertheless able to go through the 400-year Turkish occupation, one of the most brutal in history, practically keeping their identity, religion, customs, and language intact, and are extremely proud of their country and its achievements. The very word "Turk" makes the hair on the end of the most cosmopolitan Greek stand on end, although the object of their hatred is Turkey as a concept and not individual Turks.

But, there is also the other side of the coin. Living in a country that has lost more than three-quarters of its former territory and which is constantly on the verge of bankruptcy, they are burdened with a huge inferiority complex about the ancient and Byzantine Greeks, because they failed to revive the "Magna Graecia" of their forefathers. Deep down, they would welcome any opportunity to retake their "lost homeland", no matter the cost. And since the Turks, in turn, dream of reviving the Ottoman Empire, relations between these nations are very, very strained.

Except for the Turks, the Greeks bear no ill feelings towards any other nations. True, they do not particularly favor the Bulgarians, nor do they burn with love for the Albanians, who managed to profit from the Greek civil war and drag the region of Northern Epirus with half a million Greeks inhabiting it behind the communist "iron curtain".

The Greeks have a difficult relationship with each other. The Cretans ridicule the Peloponnesians, the Macedonians ridicule the Roumeliots, the inhabitants of Epirus ridicule the Thessalians, the islanders ridicule the inhabitants of mainland Greece, the Athenians ridicule everyone else, and so on until the whole country is covered. And in case it is necessary to question the mental abilities of any people, the Greeks have Pontian Greeks (immigrants from cities on the Black Sea coast). In general, there are a huge number of different jokes and anecdotes about them, for example: an announcement at the airport: "We ask the Pontians not to scatter grain along the runway. "Big Bird" will fly in anyway." And the Greek gypsies are a favorite subject of jokes, because of their penchant for theft, obsessive trading of all unnecessary little things, countless children, and unimaginable dirt.

All Greeks have a dual nature. They are the smartest, but also the vainest people, energetic, but also disorganized, with a sense of humor, but full of prejudices, hot-headed, impatient, but true fighters… One minute they fight for the truth, but the other is to hate the one who refuses to lie. They are half good - vainest and half bad, fickle, with changing moods, self-centered, eccentric, and wise people. In Georgia, the Greeks are called "berdznebi" ("sages"), and in Greece is called "saberdzeneti", that is, "land of the sages." In different strata of society, one can find Alexander the Great - noble, brave, intelligent, broad-minded, sincere, warm-hearted, and generous, and Karagöz - low, treacherous, selfish, talkative, vain, lazy, envious, and greedy - often in the same person.

The Greeks have a special relationship with the government. It is well known that most nations have the government they deserve. This couldn't be more true of the Greeks. Their successive governments - regardless of political color - usually exhibit the same shortcomings as the average Greek. Despite their undoubted intelligence, the Greeks are a very gullible people, especially when some charismatic politician tells them what they want to hear. They are ready to follow him until the moment when bitter disappointment sets in. When, of course, nothing works out for a politician, the Greeks begin to become mischievous and vote for his resignation.

Bureaucracy in Greece has been elevated to the level of an art - the art of turning citizens into enemies. In any given ministry or government institution there is some distant relative, a godfather, a godfather, or a friend of an acquaintance. He can speed up the process, sometimes as a favor, and sometimes for an appropriate bribe. A Greek who has managed, in one way or another, to become a government official, in nine cases out of ten does not consider himself a servant of society.

He becomes a kind of little dictator who is afraid to make any decisions on his own but takes pleasure in tormenting the unfortunate petitioners. Even getting a small certificate turns into a real operation, which will take several hours or even days, since you have to deal with at least half a dozen officials, which you need to walk through to get a signature from one, a stamp from another, a visa from third and so on.

Greek Character

Greece in Greek is Hellas, and the Greeks are Hellenes and Hellenids (as they call themselves). The Greeks are people of the Mediterranean, with a mild climate, caressed by the rays of the sun all year round. Like all residents of other countries around the Mediterranean Sea, they are never in a hurry, do not stress at work, do not try to "jump in over their heads," try in every possible way to evade "duties" and, in general, live for the present day. At the same time, they manage not to cross the lines of outright laziness and idleness. The spirit of competition is alien to the Greeks.

They nurture their over-inflated egos, and cherish an extreme passion for freedom of choice - which makes them completely impervious to understanding the words "discipline", "coordination" or "system". In interpreting the word "freedom" in their way, the Greeks often confused good manners with the humble obedience that they were forced to learn under the Turkish yoke to survive. They believe that politeness is only for slaves.

"I" is the favorite word of the Greeks. Absolutely every Greek considers himself the center of the universe. With all this, the southern temperament can be traced very clearly in the character of the Greeks. The Greeks are cheerful, have a wonderful sense of humor, and do everything they like with amazing passion - they have fun and sadness, talk and dance, argue, and even pray. Self-control, although invented by the ancient Spartans, is not only unknown to modern Greeks but also completely incomprehensible to them. The Greeks give full vent to their emotions, and… don't care about the consequences! They shout, scream, burst into pompous tirades, and furiously curse fate in the same way, about important and Even though not very important circumstances. No feeling is too personal to remain unexpressed. Their passions know no bounds.

Such rampant incontinence often results in a burning need to express oneself in some physical form. The brightest facet of the Greek character can be observed in dancing. All over the world people dance when they are happy. The Greeks, on the other hand, tend to pour out their deepest pain and heartache in a heart-rending, majestic dance rhythm.

The most significant Greek dance is… "sirtaki". This is the same dance that no holiday is complete without, and which has long become the hallmark of the country. Even though it is very young ("the classic" version of shirataki was invented, literally, in a few minutes by Mikis Theodorakis for the Hollywood film Jeremy Arnold "Zorba the Greek", in 1964), it absorbed many dance elements truly folk dances of the country - Cretan "pimientos" and "shirts", Athenian "Hasapiko", island "Nafpiko", continental "rebetiko" and dozens of others.

And the Greeks themselves, without regard for tourists, dance the same ancient folk dances, simply calling them "sirtaki" - for brevity and clarity to outsiders. By the way, here you can easily see the same "sirtaki" at a youth disco, or completely unimaginable dance variations at any wedding, or, which is not uncommon, at a funeral. At the same time, equally ancient musical instruments are used - the indispensable bouzouki (another calling card of the country, also revived from oblivion by the composer Mikis Theodorakis), lute, lyre, reed flute, bagpipes, mandolin, and others. And the most favorite dance of the Greeks is no, not sirtaki, but zeybekiko, similar to the dance of a drunken sailor. Performed, as a rule, by one man. The audience sits in a circle and applauds. One got tired, the next one entered the circle, and so on.

But let's not forget about the dual nature of the Greeks. The heat of the Greek temperament is organically combined with the ice of the well-known indifference of the Greeks to everything related to the improvement of public life or to any worthy cause that will not bring them personal benefit.

Greeks move and drive aggressively, and their actions are completely free from any concern for the well-being and peace of mind of others. Don't expect them to say "thank you" and "please", and don't expect Greeks to remain calm in a crisis.

A Greek cannot talk if his hands are full, he is a quiet Greek - one who can be heard no further than the next street. Two Greeks talking amicably sound like they are ready to kill each other. Greeks proclaim their views not only in countless coffee shops but also on the streets, on buses, or in minibusses. The Greeks love to listen to themselves, and when they are carried away by their rhetoric, wild exaggerations and sweeping generalizations can easily mislead. In Greece, during a conversation, it is not customary to take your eyes off your interlocutor. If a Greek "broadcasts into space," you can be sure that the conversation is about something not very important, and the interlocutor is bored.

Greece has its code of honor, and it is called "filotimo". This means generosity, hospitality, respect for others (especially elders), love of freedom, personal pride, dignity, courage, of course - a sense of humor, and a dozen other concepts. The most prominent philosophers of the country (both modern and ancient) have more than once turned to the description of the various components of "philotimo". Lies, non-repayment of debt, failure to fulfill promises - all this can become an indelible stain for life, therefore, many Greeks try to avoid such "offenses", at least about their loved ones and friends. About "strangers", petty cunning or dishonesty is "as if tolerated."

Intoxication and appearing drunk in a public place in Greece is regarded as an inability to control oneself and is by no means encouraged. Therefore, a Greek will never insist on "one more" at the table - the sense of proportion and the art of wine drinking have been elevated to a cult here since ancient times! Nobody dreams of a reputation as a drunkard in this country, and any bad act in a drunken stupor can ruin a person's whole life.

In provincial towns, even on the streets, everyone greets everyone, and often more than once a day. Handshakes are just for getting to know each other: friends say to each other "Yia sou!" and kiss on both cheeks, regardless of gender and age. Bowing and kissing hands are reserved for priests of the Greek Orthodox Church.

There are legends about the non-punctuality of the Greeks. There is only the concept of "approximate time" here at noon since the Greeks treat all time frames very loosely. Even the Greeks have their concept of the time of day - morning here is all that is before noon (that is why the greetings "kalimera" and "kalispera" have quite clear boundaries), "after lunch" comes no earlier than 17:00 - 18: 00. However, the Greeks have lunch much earlier! In Greece, dinner begins no earlier than 21:00, and the "evening" lasts long after midnight.

The schedule of most means of transport here is such a conditional concept that the mark "noon" will most likely mean "somewhere from 11:00 to 13:00", and "after 15:00" and even "or will come or not." Local flights are also not known for their punctuality, and although international flights depart and arrive more or less on time, people make jokes about the Greek national airline, for example: The plane is about to land in New York, and the pilot asks the dispatcher about the local time. "If you are Delta," he answers, "the time is fourteen zero-zero, if you are Air France, it is two o'clock, and if you are Olympic Airways, today is Tuesday."

No other country in the world can boast so many different types of coffee shops, cafes, cafeterias, taverns, restaurants, bars, nightclubs, and bouzouki venues - all of which are crowded with visitors seven days a week. Throughout the country you will not find a city square that on a sunny day would not be filled with tables and chairs, lounging on which, the majority of the country's population while away the time in idleness, as if tomorrow would never come. And Greeks also love coffee. With ice.

Eating out is a favorite pastime for Greeks, especially if the restaurant they choose has a show or live music. The Greek idea of the best way to spend an evening is to sit down at a tavern table, preferably with two or three married couples (sometimes with children), then they begin to eat excessively, drink moderately, and talk a lot until late into the night. , while children have fun pulling street cats by the tails, or simply fall asleep from fatigue on chairs. Greeks are not aggressive. There are almost no fights in bars. At most, they will shout and wave their hands, after a while, they will calm down and communicate as if nothing had happened.

The Greeks not only produce a lot of tobacco - they also smoke a lot of it. Smoking is seen as a sign of "modernity", and given the famous Greek indulgence, it is already difficult for adults to break an established habit. At the same time, the total life expectancy of Greeks is about 79 years for men, and women live slightly longer - up to 82 years.

Greeks don't like to work. Greece has 12 official holidays, plus 22 working days of paid leave. And also weekends, sick leave, mandatory various strikes - all this allows an enterprising Greek, for about six months, to do what he loves most in the world - that is, do nothing. As a result, during the two weeks around Christmas and the Easter holidays, as well as during the two hottest summer months - July and August - life in the country comes to a standstill.

None of the Greeks consider themselves a sinner, everyone is convinced that when they die they will go to heaven, and everyone believes in an afterlife (moreover, in a good and comfortable life). When they die, Greeks rest in marble graves topped with large white marble crosses. Three years after burial, the bones are dug up and placed in family tombs, thus solving the problem of overcrowding in cemeteries. Flowers, fresh or artificial, and constantly burning oil lamps in intricate glass lanterns are standard decorations for graves.

Greek Hospitality

"Xenos" in Greek means both "foreigner" and "guest". Already in the time of Homer, hospitality in Greece was not only a kind of ritual, with slight religious overtones, but also turned into a form of art. The Greeks were the world's first "xenophiles" - that is, they loved friendly strangers.

The Greeks are incredibly hospitable people. They love guests very much and love to visit themselves. For a Greek, a guest is something sacred. Unlike many neighboring countries, in Greece it is customary to receive guests in your own home, and not in a cafe or restaurant, although the latter is not uncommon.

Receiving guests is associated with an endless series of customs and rituals. Well, for example, the Greeks, by the character of the first guest, judge what the day, week, or year will be like: if a calm person comes, that means there will be a quiet period, noisy and fiery, that means everything will be fun, and so on.

Nothing is impossible if you decide to come as a guest to a Greek home. You will become an ideal guest if you follow a minimum number of simple rules. For example, you should not cross the threshold of a house with your right foot (especially in the provinces they pay attention to this), you should wish something good to the whole house and its owners at the entrance, bring a small gift with you, and, of course, behave with dignity at the table. Flowers, sweets, or wine are perfect gifts and remember, in Greece, it is not customary to open gifts in front of guests.

Be sure to praise the hostess or cook - for a Greek, a person who knows how to cook deliciously is often almost a saint, therefore, any praise addressed to them will be received with special enthusiasm. The main thing here is not to overdo it! Everything else is quite European.

A Greek feast is always a feast and a whole set of various traditional elements that a foreigner still won't remember the first time. The presentation of dishes, their order and set - all this has its meaning and meaning for a Greek. Often lunch or dinner is quickly moved or even initially organized in the fresh air - in the yard, on the veranda. You must be prepared that as the feast progresses, more and more guests will join - both invited and those who "dropped in for a sneak peek." Therefore, for almost half of the evening, you will have to greet and get to know someone. So don't be surprised if, when you visit a Greek friend, by the end of the evening you will have met half the village! It's the custom here, they know everything about everyone and communicate often.

The table manners of the Greeks leave much to be desired. Elbows scurry back and forth, hitting neighboring plates; your neighbor may run into your shoulder in an unequal struggle with a stubborn piece of meat. People reach into shared dishes with appetizers and salads with their fingers and dip individual pieces of bread into the common sauce. At the same time, everyone is chatting and chewing without closing their mouths. But they more than compensate for their "manners" with a good mood and lively sociability.

Greeks often like to organize a feast in a restaurant or tavern. Sometimes it seems that all Greek men do is sit in cafes and drink. This is not entirely true: Greeks often drop into such establishments, but rarely stay there for a long time, only in the evenings noisy groups of friends and acquaintances gather here. Any cafe is a meeting place, a point for exchanging news and settling matters, and only then an establishment where you can drink and sit.

This is the main place where any Greek man learns the latest gossip, meets business partners, friends, and relatives, and often receives guests or celebrates festive events. As a rule, if a Greek invites someone to dinner, he pays the bill. It is wrong to offer to contribute to the payment of the bill, since for a resident the inability to pay his bill is humiliating. It is interesting that Greeks almost always pay bills in a tavern or restaurant only in cash. By the way, the word "symposium" translated from ancient Greek means "drinking together."

Many tourists in Greece note the inattention of waiters to a lonely visitor. This is not due to their laziness or unwillingness to serve you, but precisely to the tradition of this country of visiting taverns in large groups. The Greeks believe that if one person is sitting at a table, then he is simply waiting for the company - then the menu and everything else will be offered, but for now, it is simply pointless to waste time and effort on it. However, the natural slowness of the Greeks still takes place here.

As in all Mediterranean countries, the ritual of siesta, or afternoon rest, is sacredly observed in Greece. From 14:00 - 15:00 to 17:00 - 18:00, some establishments simply do not work, and those that are open have a reduced staff. During these hours it is not customary to make appointments, make phone calls, or simply make noise.

Greek Language

Today, Greece is united by 13 million people, most of whom live in Greece, the rest in Cyprus, Albania, and in Greek communities around the world.

The language came to the modern Greek version through centuries of transformation due to political and linguistic factors.

Stages of language development

The history of the Greek language is divided into periods:

Proto-Greek —no written texts from this period, nor an example of an alphabet, survive. However archaeological and historical finds prove that the Greek language system appeared more than 30 centuries ago.

Mycenaean Greek was the language of the Mycenaean civilization (16th century BC). At the same time, the first Greek writing appeared, which today is known as Linear B.

Classical (or Ancient Greek) Greek is the language known through-out the Roman Empire. It is considered the language of the classical period of Greek civilization (VI-IV centuries BC).

At this time, the territory of Greece was divided into many states, each of which spoke its dialect.

Athens later became the political, economic, and cultural center of the Greek world, so the local dialect was used as a common language.

But gradually the dialects of different regions mixed, and a new variant of the dialect appeared - Koine.

In the ancient Greek period, great writers worked on their works: Homer, Sappho, Plato, Aristotle, and Aristophanes. It was during this time that many of the central works of Greek literature were written, including the Iliad and the Odyssey.

Koine is a Greek dialect that emerged from the mixing of several dialects. It lived for several centuries and later became the official language of the Roman Empire. Koine is considered the original language of the New Testament and the basis of modern Greek.

Medieval (Byzantine) Greek was the literary language of Byzantium. It was spoken until the fall of the Byzantine Empire in the 15th century AD.

Modern Greek, the language spoken by Greeks today. Most regions of Greece have local spoken dialects and accents.

For centuries, Greek was the lingua franca of the ancient world in the Mediterranean region. It was the language of culture and trade. No educated Roman could do without the Greek language, and therefore, thousands of words penetrated Latin and from there passed into modern European languages. In the English language alone, about a third of the total vocabulary is either words of Greek origin or transcriptions from Greek. In addition to medical, scientific, and literary terms, as well as hundreds of names of plants, animals, and chemical elements, words of Greek origin in modern language are represented in the range from "auto" to "iamb".

Modern Greek (or modern Greek) is quite different from ancient Greek and has undergone major changes over the centuries. The Greeks are very proud of their language (Greeks, in general, are proud of everything Greek), characterizing this by the fact that they speak the language of Homer, but in fact, modern Greeks would not be able to understand Homer. The thing is that in the modern Greek language, there are many more Slavic or Turkish word forms than ancient ones. In addition, different local dialects are used in different regions of Greece, for example: "Sfakia" - in Crete, "Tsakonika" - in the east and center of the Peloponnese, "Sarakitsani" - in the mountainous regions, Vlachian - in the northwestern regions, etc. Further.

In addition to territorial affiliation, the dialects of the Modern Greek language should also be distinguished by ethnic groups, for example: "Romaniote" ("Greek Yiddish"), "Arvanitika" (Albanian), Macedonian, Rumean and Pontic (the languages of the Greeks of the Black Sea region, which returned in the 90s to their historical homeland), Pomak (Bulgarian, with an admixture of Turkish words), Cypriot, Gypsy, Turkish and so on. And it cannot be otherwise, in this historical cauldron, from time immemorial, too many nationalities have been "cooked".

The Greek language, in general, is very beautiful, too exotic and soft for prim Europe. And not at all easy to learn. Additional difficulties in the perception of this beautiful language are its division into 2 separate branches: the "pure" ("kafarevusu") form of Modern Greek until the beginning of the 20th century, and the simpler one – "demotics" (colloquial version). "Demotics", which absorbed many colloquial words and borrowings from Italian, Turkish, and Slavic languages, served as the basis of the modern language.

However, in the second half of the twentieth century, an intensified revival of "kafarevusa" began, so to speak, the artificial cleansing of the Greek language from foreign words, which gave rise to considerable problems. "Demotics", however, has retained its folk basis and is used in schools, on the radio, on television, and in most newspapers. However, the church and jurisprudence still use their forms of "kafarevusa", which can already be safely considered independent dialects, since many Greek emigrants do not understand them.

Greek grammar is quite complex: nouns are divided into three genders, all with different singular and plural endings. All adjectives and verbs must agree with nouns in gender and number. In general, Greek, according to its rules, is very similar to the Russian language, and this similarity only complicates auditory perception.

Accepted forms of Greek greeting: "kyrie" - "lord", "kyrie" - "lady". Depending on the time of day, the greetings "kalimera" ("good morning", "good afternoon") and "calispera" ("good evening") is used. Thank you sounds like "Ineucha" in Greek. You should know that "ne" in Greek means "yes", and "no" means "ohi". They also shake their heads incorrectly.

When answering in the negative, the Greek slightly nods his head from bottom to top (as we mean "yes"), and not from side to side (in this case he wants to show that he does not understand). A wave with an outstretched palm in the interlocutor's face means an extreme degree of indignation, a rotation of the palm means surprise, and so on. In general, the gestures and body language of residents are sometimes no less expressive than speech, therefore, body language here is considered a very important component of conversation. But the meaning of many of them, at times, is very different from those accepted in our country.

The Greeks themselves are very respectful of foreigners' attempts to learn at least a few words in Greek. Tourists who know a few Greek words automatically move from the category of idle visitor ("turistas") to the more "noble" category of guest ("xenos" or "xeni").

Religion of Greece

Religion occupied an important place in ancient Greek culture. However, unlike the Egyptians, the Greeks dressed their gods in human clothing. It was important for them to enjoy life. The Greeks imagined that from chaos the earth, darkness, and night were born, and then light, ether, day, sky, sea, and other great forces of nature. From heaven and earth, the older generation of gods was born, and from them Zeus and the other Olympian gods. Sacrifices were made to the Olympian gods. It was believed that gods, like people, needed food. The Greeks also believed that the shadows of the dead needed food, and tried to feed them. Each temple had its, own priest, and the main temples had an oracle. He predicted the future or reported what the Olympian gods said.

Chronologically, the emergence of Christianity can be dated back to the middle of the 2nd century AD. From the ashes of the Greco-Roman pantheon, a more mature idea of monotheism arose, moreover, the idea of a god-man who accepted martyrdom for the sake of our salvation. Due to the official non-recognition of Christianity at the very beginning of its existence, adherents of the new faith were forced to gather secretly. Over a thousand years, Christianity has evolved from scattered underground societies to one of the most important forces influencing the development of civilizations.

By the 8th century, the Pope and the Patriarch of Constantinople began to argue over many issues relating to religion. One of the many differences of opinion is the celibacy of the clergy (priests in Rome must remain celibate, whereas an Orthodox priest can marry before his ordination). Also, there are some differences in the food during fasting or in the wording of some prayers. Disputes and objections between the spiritual leaders of Orthodoxy and Catholicism became increasingly intense, and in 1054 the Patriarch and the Pope finally parted ways with each other. The Orthodox Church and the Roman Catholic Church have each taken their, and, path of development: this division is called heresy. Today, Orthodoxy is the national religion of Greece.

All Greeks are Orthodox. Moreover, this is a religious nation. The role of the Orthodox Church in the life of the average Greek is difficult to overestimate. The Greek Orthodox Church is under the jurisdiction of the Ecumenical Patriarch and, according to the constitution, the church is separated from the state, however, at least half of the priests' salaries are paid by the state.

The priest is a highly respected person in the local community; most Greeks cannot imagine a wedding or funeral ceremony without a church, and there is nothing to say about baptism or Easter. In Greece, there is a law allowing civil marriage, and it has been in effect since 1982, however, until now, 95% of couples get married in a church. There are always images hanging in every home, and they can be seen in almost all offices, shops, and even on buses or taxis. In many schools, the school year begins with the blessing of the priest, and in some, they also teach the Law of God.

In every Greek family, church customs and sacraments are strictly observed, and are taken very seriously. The most common time to attend services is Sunday. When passing or driving past churches, every Greek believer is sure to cross himself. Such major religious holidays as Christmas, Epiphany, and Easter turn into mass festivities in Greece.

Each city, commune, trading community, or church has "its own Saint" and a special feast day in his honor, which usually turns into a "panegyric" - a religious and cultural festival in which various church services, banquets, music, and dance performances are held. Most Greeks do not celebrate their birthday, but the day of "their" Saint, in honor of whom they were named, certainly does. Greek ingenuity even brought into the ranks of the Saints pagan gods, like Dionysus or the ancient philosophers Socrates and Plato, and therefore there are many reasons for celebrations here.

The religion of Greece is present in many different aspects of Greek society. The Orthodox Church also influences some political issues and every time a new decision is made that does not satisfy the Orthodox leaders, it is always accompanied by disapproval from church representatives.

What about Orthodoxy? Greece is one of the recognized world centers of monastic life. Only in this country (and nowhere else in the world) does there exist a separate theocratic male state of Athos, where only men live (women can never (!) set foot on this land - those who disobey face a long prison sentence) and only monks (although not all are Greek by origin). Also, one of the cult places of Greece is the famous Meteora monasteries, built on rocks.

Despite their incredible piety, the Greeks are also incredibly super-stitious people. In Greece, everyone believes in the power of the evil eye; you will not meet a child who would not wear, as an amulet, a turquoise bead, sometimes with an eye drawn on it. For the same reason, turquoise beads adorn the necks of horses and donkeys in villages. A Greek would never dare to praise someone's elegance and beauty, especially children, without spitting three times and knocking on wood. This is done to ward off the envy of the gods when you praise someone.

It is considered bad luck not to offer something to drink to anyone who comes to their house, regardless of the time of day. On the Saturday before Easter, a plate will be broken "for good luck" (this symbolizes the rejection of death), and the same ritual will be performed at the wedding. The sacrifice of a lamb is an integral part of many Christian holidays in the country, just as it was many centuries ago, in the times of completely different gods. However, what else can you expect in a country where the Parthenon still stands Olympus rises, and almost a third of the mountains and valleys bear the names of ancient gods?

Greek Clothing

The fashion and clothing of Ancient Greece were distinguished by five features: regularity, organization, proportionality, symmetry, and expediency. In ancient culture, the human body was first viewed as a mirror reflecting the unity and perfection of the world. Even during the archaic period, Greek women's clothing was distinguished by its slender lines created by flowing fabrics.

2

Processes of Democratization in Ancient Greece

T he publishing house of the National Research University Higher School of Economics published a book by Valery Gushchin, Associate Professor of the Department of Humanities at the National Research University Higher School of Economics - Perm, "Athens on the Path to Democracy: 8th–5th Centuries BC." The monograph examines the process of formation of Athenian democracy during the archaic and classical periods. One of the significant incentives for the emergence of democracy was the struggle for power and influence within the aristocracy. We are publishing a book fragment showing the processes that became the starting point for democratization.

The Aristocracy of Athens: Appearance and Role

What was the Athenian aristocracy and how did it arise? It can be assumed that there is a close connection between the aristocracy and the military sphere of social life. Initially, martial arts were the lot of the aristocracy in the military sphere, but at the turn of the 8th–7th centuries. BC. As some authors believe, aristocratic status begins to be determined by cavalry. This conclusion is most often made due to the obvious connection between aristocratic status and equestrianism. However, historical facts cast doubt on this postulate, since the existence of cavalry in archaic Athens is not recorded.

If this is so, then the fate of the aristocracy should be associated with the phalanx that appeared in these same centuries. The phalanx is traditionally believed to have had a democratizing effect on aristocratic society. Perhaps this was so since the phalanx objectively strengthened the role of those representatives of the demos who were wealthy enough to acquire hoplite weapons. But it is unlikely that the phalanx could reduce the role of the aristocracy, which found a place for itself here too - in the front ranks of the fighting (promachoi).

In other words, in the 8th century. BC. we can talk about the emergence of an aristocracy. At the beginning and middle of the 8th century. BC. burials appear that can be called aristocratic (for example, the Ceramics cemetery and the Dipilon burials).

A feature of this period is the appearance of rich burials not only in Athens but also in Attica. Consequently, we can talk about the emergence of an aristocracy, both Athenian and peripheral. It can be assumed that internal colonization, the emergence of new settlements, as well as the formation of a peripheral aristocracy could not help but weaken pre-existing social and political ties and even lead to decentralization. Formally, the urban and political center, which was Athens, existed, but the connections between the center and the periphery could be weakened. Let us refer to Thucydides, who, talking about the cynicism of Theseus, noted that "... the Athenians lived for a long time, enjoying autonomy, in different parts of their country" (Th uc. II. 16. 1, hereinafter trans. F Mishchenko).

> *In the political sphere, the emancipation of the aristocracy was manifested in the fact that royal power was replaced by a collective magistracy - a college of nine archons, who, according to tradition, from 684/3 BC. began to be elected for a term of one year. The archons included the eponymous archon, basileus, polemarch and six thesmothetes.*

The eponymous archon (or simply archon) in this list was perhaps the most significant magistracy. As representatives of the executive branch, the archons were vested with significant judicial powers. "The archons," according to Aristotle, "had the right to decide matters definitively, and not, as now, to carry out only a preliminary investigation" (Arist. Ath. Pol. 3.5). The polemarchs led the army, the basileus dealt with religious issues, and they were in charge of murder trials. The last on this list was a commission of aesthetes, whose task was to record the decisions made. It is possible that these were decisions of the mentioned officials and judicial verdicts passed by the Areopagites.

Mechanism of political domination

In order to concretely imagine the mechanism of political domination during the archaic period, let us consider the personal composition of the archons. From the period preceding Solon's reforms, we know the names of 24 officials, of whom 19 were eponymous archons. They were all representatives of noble families, although it is quite difficult to establish their belonging to one or another family or group.

Among the famous people we mentioned, Dracon stands apart, with whose name tradition associates the change in legislation, calling him thesmothetus, i.e. legislator (Paus. IX. 36. 8). curiously, it is he (if we consider Draco a real person), and not the highest official - in this case, the archon-eponym Aristekhmus - who introduces new laws (Arist. Ath. Pol. 4. 1).

So, what can be said about the political significance of the archons? Charles Hignett, speaking about the state structure of Athens in the ancient period, notes that the position of archons during this period was the main object of political ambitions and party struggle.

Confirmation can be found in Aristotle, who, however, talks about the situation that arose after Solon's reforms. Difficulties in electing an archon, which arose shortly after Solon's departure from Athens, as well as Damasius's attempt to retain this position by force, led Aristotle to suggest that "the archon had very great power, since, apparently, there was a constant struggle over this position" (Arist. Ath. Pol. 13.2). However, it should be borne in mind that the author himself expresses this idea extremely carefully.

The above analysis of the personal composition of the archons allows us to make several assumptions. On the one hand, we see among the archons representatives of quite influential families - the Philaids, and Alkmeonids. The former is even more common among archons than others. This is certainly evidence of the influence of the Philaids. But does this indicate the importance of the position itself? What is striking is that among the characters mentioned, there are almost no famous people. Those who were not related to the position of archon gained great fame - for example, Phrynon, Draco.

It seems that the eponymous archons were more nominal leaders than truly influential politicians. Therefore, we consider it possible to join the opinion of those researchers who believe that the importance of the position of archon in the period under review was hardly great.

A one-year master's degree was unlikely to become a politically significant position. Although the archons may have been the leaders of aristocratic hysteria (like Megacles, who suppressed the rebellion of Cylon, as discussed below), we believe that this magistracy was most likely the initial step in a political career, since it opened the way to the Areopagus.

The role of the people

Demos was indeed removed from the management of state affairs, i.e. the role of the people's assembly was insignificant. In confirmation of this, let us mention the previously cited passage of the "Athenian Polity", according to which the demos "had no share in anything" (Arist. Ath. Pol. 2.2). The latter should be understood as an indication of the political lack of rights of the demos.

The role of the popular masses in making political decisions was revealed only from time to time - at moments of intensification of the political struggle or during spontaneous gatherings of armed people. This was the case, in particular, during the suppression of the Quilon conspiracy. Thucydides says that the Athenians, tired of the long siege, went home, obliging nine archons to conduct the siege and giving them unlimited powers (Th uc. I. 126. 8). In the last words one can hear echoes of a political, collectively made decision. The community of armed Athenians besieging Cylon apparently turned into an impromptu popular assembly. But this was the exception rather than the rule. Spontaneously occurring public gatherings turned into impromptu public assemblies only in extraordinary cases.

Informal Power: The Beginning of the Struggle

Looking for the most influential institute or magistracy in the archaic period is hardly justified. Most likely, real political power was exercised informally, i.e. outside political institutions. It was possessed by representatives of the noblest or influential clans or families, who relied on their political groupings (hysteria). Noteworthy are the words of Aristotle that in oligarchic regimes, election to the highest government positions was conditioned by a high property qualification or belonging to an aristocratic heteria (Arist. Pol. V. 1305 b 30–35). Consequently, a necessary condition for political influence was belonging to the dominant political group - heteria.

In form, heteria was a community of friends and companions. Most often, its members are people of the same age and social status. This was exactly what, say, the heteria Cylon was like, uniting, according to Herodotus, peers of the same age (Herod. V. 71). At the head of each of these heterias was an influential figure - a leader. The leader, one might say, was its integrating factor. We believe that not every representative of an aristocratic family could become a leader. Most likely, he became the scion of an influential family or the eldest in age. About Cylon, for example, Thucydides says that he was a representative of an ancient and influential family (τῶν πάλαι εὐγενής τε καὶ δυνατός) (Th uc. I. 126. 3). In addition, his leadership was strengthened by his marriage to the daughter of the Megarian tyrant Theagenes.

On this basis, we can assume a lack of equality within the aristocracy, i.e. a kind of ranking of its representatives.

As a result, let us repeat our earlier assumption: the leaders of aristocratic groups could be called hegemons. However, in the archaic period one can hardly expect the existence of developed socio-political terminology. The basis of the heteria, of course, were aristocrats (and perhaps not only them), connected by ties of friendship. To a greater extent, what connected the participants of the heteria resembled family ties. It is known that friendship among the Greeks also meant, among other things, symmachia (military alliance).

It is known that the archaic period was a time of fierce struggle between the aristocracy and aristocratic heterae for power and influence. The reason for the aggravation of political confrontation was that power was exercised, as we said above, informally. This meant that the mechanism for changing political leaders either did not exist or was simply not used.

This type of power relations can be characterized as a crisis, since it was fraught with serious socio-political upheavals that posed a threat to the entire society. In addition, new features are appearing in political life and, in particular, a tendency towards oligarchization - the seizure and desire to retain power by representatives of more influential families (clans), relying on their own groups.

For the first time, we see hysteria and its leader fighting for power at the time of Cylon's conspiracy (Th uc. I. 126)78. It makes sense to take a closer look at these events. "There was a certain Cylon in Athens," says Herodotus, "a winner at Olympia. He became so proud that he began to seek tyranny. With a bunch of his peers, he tried to capture the Acropolis. When he failed, Cylon sat down as if "begging for protection" at the idol of the goddess. The elders (in the original "pritans" - V.G.) navkrari, who then ruled in Athens, persuaded Cylon and his comrades to leave there, promising to save their lives" (Herod. V. 71, trans. G. Stratanovsky). And then something unexpected happened, and the conspirators were killed. At the same time, the blame for the murder of the "begging" fell on the Alcmaeonids.

If we talk about further historical events, then after the suppression of the Quilon conspiracy, we observe a grueling struggle between influential political clans or families. The conspiracy, and especially the brutality of its suppression, had a significant impact on the political landscape.

As a result of the reprisal against the failed tyrant, and most importantly, as a result of the "desecration" of the Alcmaeonids - the murder of the conspirators - the balance in society and the ruling group, the core of which may have been the Alcmaeonids, was lost. Plutarch reports that the main struggle was between them and the supporters of Cylon. "The surviving accomplices of Cylon," writes Plutarch, "again entered into force and were constantly at enmity with the party of Megacles" (Plut. Sol. 12). And this was no longer so much a rivalry between the aristocracy seeking power and influence, but rather a struggle for destruction. The result of the suppression of Cylon's conspiracy was, perhaps, that the Athenian aristocracy split into two opposing factions: supporters and opponents of the Alcmaeonids.

The suppression of Cylon's conspiracy and the subsequent struggle thoroughly shook Athenian society. Following this, naturally, attempts are made to stabilize the situation. If Draco's legislation is associated with the situation that developed in Athens after the suppression of Cylon's conspiracy, then it can be considered one of such attempts to restore the lost balance. However, these measures did not bring the desired result.

The expulsion of the Alcmaeonids significantly influenced the political situation in Attica. On the one hand, the removal of a clan that did not belong to the most ancient and indigenous Attic clans strengthened the traditional agricultural aristocracy, i.e. those who could conventionally be called Eupatrides. But, on the other hand, the removal, one might say, saved the reputation of the Alcmaeonids, since they were not among those greedy aristocrats who enslaved unpaid debtors, i.e. a considerable part of the Athenian demos.

The expulsion of the Alcmaeonids did not bring the expected calm. True, now the contradictions between the aristocracy and the demos are coming to the fore. At the turn of the 7th–6th centuries. BC. A severe political and socio-economic crisis broke out in Attica, calling into question the very way of exercising power. The result of the rule of the aristocracy was not only a political but also a socio-economic crisis caused by the enslavement of farmers on an unprecedented scale.

3

The Gods and Mythology

The gods of Ancient Greece are mythical heroes who should be perceived as interesting literary characters and, of course, an important part of world history and culture. Over time, the attitude towards mythology transformed and, if Hesiod and Pindar considered everything that they wrote about the Greek gods to be true, and the ancient Greek tragedians treated their works as religious texts that claimed to be true, then later mythology became a literary work.

The gods of Ancient Greece are very similar to people. They are jealous and suffer, they are vindictive and cruel, they make ridiculous mistakes, and they are often distinguished from humans only by a number of supernatural abilities. This is how pantheism often represents higher beings . Many gods cannot be perfect at once.

We learned about many ancient gods thanks to the literary works of Ancient times that have come down to us. The list of authors with whom we can familiarize ourselves is short, which is not surprising. Many manuscripts may simply not have reached us. Everyone knows Homer - the Iliad and the Odyssey. Many have read Hesiod's Theogony, as well as Works and Days, where the gods also play a role. Pindar, the lyrical ancient Greek poet, constantly touches on the theme of the gods of Ancient Greece. The author of comedies, Aristophanes, turns to mythological subjects.

And even the traveler and writer Pausanias, who lived in the 2nd century. n. e. still takes myths quite seriously, describing them as some kind of religious truth.

Gods of Ancient Greece (Olympus)

It is impossible to imagine the ancient Greek divine pantheon without its main characters - the gods of Olympus. This is not the first generation of divine entities in the imagination of the ancient Greeks. The gods did not arise on their own. They had Mother Earth and Father Sky, who gave birth to the Titans. The Titans became the fathers of the gods. The Olympic gods are the grandchildren of the very first and most important deities. But they were the ones closest to people, because in their minds they had the same weaknesses and vices.

All 12 Greek gods were related to each other (and quite close):

- Zeus (Jupiter) is the head of the dynasty.
- His two brothers: are Poseidon (Neptune) and Hades (Pluto).
- Sister: Hestia (Vesta).
- Hera (Juno) - wife of Zeus.
- Ares (Mars) - son of Zeus and Hera.
- Other children of Zeus:
- Athena (Minerva), Apollo, Aphrodite (Venus), Hermes (Mercury), and Artemis (Diana).
- Son of Hera:

- Hephaestus (Vulcan). Whether he is also the son of Zeus is a moot point.

Greek gods often entered into different relationships with people; such "mixed" unions often became the causes of tragedies, which are full of ancient Greek mythology.

Zeus was considered the most important god . In the Iliad, the father of the family does not hesitate to praise himself:

…go ahead, try, gods, and be convinced of everything: Having now lowered the golden chain from the high sky, All to the last god and all to the last goddess Hang on to it; but you will not be able to drag Zeus, the builder of the highest, from heaven to earth, no matter how much you work! If, having judged for good, I desire to draw it, I will draw it with the earth itself and with the sea itself, And with my right hand I will wrap a chain around the top of Olympus; and the entire universe will hang on high - So much higher than the gods and so much higher than mortals!

This does not prevent Zeus from acting as a traitor, from being a vengeful god; in addition, his omnipotence is in great doubt: other gods are constantly deceiving him.

His wife Hera, the patroness of marriage, was also Zeus' sister. She was raised by the titans Oceanus and Tethys. In addition to taking revenge on Zeus's many lovers, she also punishes their children. The truth in the myth of the Golden Fleece also shows its positive qualities - it protects the heroes.

Hades didn't have a good reputation either. He kidnaps his wife

Persephone to make him queen of the underworld. It is mistakenly believed that Hades was the god of death; Hades commanded the dead, but death itself was personified by the god Thanatos. Hades got something of a managerial role.

The beloved daughter of Zeus, the warrior goddess Athena, was born without the participation of a woman. She magically emerged from her father's head as an adult. Zeus loved her, she commanded lightning and had the same bad character as her father.

The healer god Apollo, who, according to myths, passed on the art of healing to people, evokes some sympathy. He was handsome and did not utter a word of lies. It was believed that he was kind and merciful to people. Nevertheless, in several myths he can be seen as cruel and merciless, but the good beginning in him still won, which cannot be said about his sister Artemis.

Artemis , the goddess of the dark moon, was also considered the patroness of "dark" affairs. Torn between good and evil, she never chose which principle would win in her. This is one of the most controversial characters in Greek mythology.

The goddess of love and beauty, Aphrodite, is mainly engaged in seduction, and even those who should not (for example, sages) fall under her spell. Homer considers her the daughter of Zeus, but in later myths we see the assumption that Aphrodite emerged from the "foam of the sea."

One of Homer's hymns says:

...on the polyphonic waves

In the form of the air, the breath of Zephyr drove her

With its wet strength. And Ora in golden diadems,

Having joyfully met the goddess, they dressed her with imperishable clothes...

They led us to the eternal gods.

And, greeting Cypris, gods

They shook her right hand, and everyone lit up with desire

Make her your legal wife and bring her into your home,

I was immensely amazed at the sight of violet-crowned Cytharea.

Her husband (according to the Odyssey), the god of fire and the blacksmith god Hephaestus, was considered to have an unsightly appearance (the only one of all the gods of Olympus). Nevertheless, although he is a stupid character, he is good-natured and loved by people. According to some myths, Hera, the god of fire, Hephaestus, gave birth to spite Zeus, who himself gave birth to Athena. Other myths consider him the son of Zeus. The Greeks did not achieve unity on this issue.

The other gods were not friendly and were vicious (each in their own way). The god of war Ares in the Iliad appears cruel and evil, vile and cowardly. In addition, one of the myths calls him Aphrodite's lover.

Other gods of Olympus

In addition to the twelve supreme gods, even less influential gods lived on Olympus:

- God of love Eros (we often know him in the role of Cupid);
- God of passion Himerot;
- God of the wedding Hymen;
- Goddess of Youth Hebe;
- Goddess of the rainbow Iris;
- Three sisters of Harita, who care for music, grace, art;
- Lovely muses.

Apollo - god of the arts, poetry, and healing

Apollo (in ancient Roman mythology - Phoebus) is the beloved son of Zeus, enchanting with his beauty and talents. He became equally famous for both his ability to play the lyre (kefir) and his dexterity in archery. Both of these objects became integral symbols of the god of arts when creating sculptures and frescoes in his honor.

Among other things, Apollo is depicted as a young, stately youth with golden curls and a clean face without a beard, which is not particularly characteristic of the appearance of the gods of Olympus. His head is decorated with a wreath of laurel leaves, as a sign of the winner - in a fistfight, Apollo surpassed the god of war Ares.

Also, incited by the desire for revenge, he defeated the mighty serpent Python, but for this act the patron of the arts was punished by his father with an eight-year exile to the human world, where he was supposed to herd sheep.

Ares - god of war

Ares is the son of Zeus and Hera, born after the battle with the Titans. In Greek mythology, he is known for his cruelty towards all living things and impulsiveness: the god of war patronized bloodshed and a ruthless attitude towards enemies.

The image of Ares is known from numerous statues and images of this resident of Olympus. So, he is a stern-looking man with developed muscles, a predatory look, and a cruel expression on his face. His figure can be sharpened with protective armor or appear half-naked, and his face can be with or without a beard.

The obligatory attributes of Ares are a spear (less often a sword), a warrior's helmet, and a burning torch. Next to the god of war, there are always assistants: a dog and a kite, which are harbingers of battle and tormented warriors who died in battle.

Artemis – goddess of the hunt

Artemis is the virginal young goddess of the hunt and fertility. Just like her twin brother Apollo, she was skilled in archery. Along with her brother, she was considered the personification of a heavenly body (the sun corresponded to Apollo, and the moon to Artemis).

Athena – goddess of wisdom and war

Born from the head of Zeus, the ancient Greek goddess Athena patronized just war, sciences, and the main crafts of the ancient world: weaving, pottery, and needlework. According to myths, she favored the Greeks during the Trojan War, and being a wise strategist and tactician, she gave the soldiers tips that led to victory.

Aphrodite – goddess of love and beauty

Ancient sources describe the Olympian goddess Aphrodite as a young, half-naked girl with a bandage around her hips. She was considered the patronage of youth, and therefore the main accessory that the goddess of beauty holds in her hands is a bowl full of wine.

The Greeks believed that by drinking a magical drink from this cup, one could gain eternal youth and forever prevent the withering of a person's natural beauty.

Lovers, musicians, and poets prayed to the goddess of love. Her very name is shrouded in legends and lyrical speculation; for example, it is believed that Aphrodite's mother was sea foam.

Nemesis - goddess of retribution

Nemesis is the all-seeing goddess of fair retribution for the evil committed by people. Ancient sources are not unanimous in determining the parents of Nemesis: the goddess of the night Nyukta and Kronos or Ocean, Themis, and Zeus, as an option - the deified incarnation of the wife of the Spartan king Tyndareus Leda after death.

The winged Nemesis is depicted on a chariot drawn by griffins (symbols of swiftness), with a sword and whip in her hands for punishment, and scales indicating justice. In the temple of Nemesis in Rhamnunt, the goddess appears with a wheel and an arm bent at the elbow - the ancient Greek measure of length - signs of the inevitability of punishment for those who neglect the fate determined by the gods and violate the laws of existence.

Helios - the sun god

The solar deity Helios, nicknamed after his father the Titan Hyperion - Hyperionides, took daily walks across the sky, driving a golden chariot drawn by four golden horses. The ancient Greeks attributed to this mythical character the ability to see all the actions that occur both on earth and on Olympus and therefore believed that the sun god was equally capable of punishing the guilty with blindness. Connected with this are appeals to the sun, as a witness to some incident.

When depicting Helios, they use the image of a young man holding a cornucopia and a ball in his hands. The statue of the Colossus of Rhodes is also created in the image of the sun god, and the island of Rhodes was donated to Helios by Zeus because, after the overthrow of the Titans, he was not invited to participate in the division of the universe.

Hemera - goddess of the day

In ancient cosmogonies, daylight and night darkness did not depend on the sun. In particular, it was believed that the celestial body accompanies the day, but its source is not the Sun, but the goddess of the day, Hemera.

In mythology, she appears as a beautiful girl, dressed in an iridescent outfit of blue and gold material. The goddess of Greece begins her journey across the sky with the dispersal of fog, the dark veil of which was thrown over the sky the day before by the mother of the goddess - Nyukta, the patroness of the night.

Hera - goddess of family ties

Hera is included in the list of twelve main Olympic deities and therefore often appears in various myths of Ancient Greece.

The wife of the thunderer Zeus protects women during childbirth and patronizes marriage, while showing power and jealousy bordering on cruelty, and is often capable of treachery towards her husband and his children from other women.

According to ancient Greek mythology, the goddess Hera created the institution of marriage, gradually crowding out polygamy from the lives of spouses. When describing this deity, they use the image of a woman with big eyes and beautiful hair.

The attributes she uses include a veil and a tiara, as symbols of chastity and the status of the wife. There are also images of the goddess with a scepter equipped with a cuckoo (with the help of this bird, Zeus deceived Hera into marriage).

Hermes - god of trade, messenger of Zeus

The ancient Greek Olympian Hermes was considered the god of commerce, wealth, travel, and also the patron of thieves. Being a messenger and messenger from the top of Olympus, as well as for leading the souls of the dead to the kingdom of the dead, he received the nickname Psychopomp - "leader of the soul."

Hermes was the brightest and most mischievous representative of the Olympian gods. So, while still a baby, he became famous for stealing sacred cows from his brother Apollo, and for his ingenuity: branches were tied to the animals' legs, hiding hoof prints on the road. Since the cunning man was later able to convince Zeus not to punish him, Hermes began to be considered the patron of rhetoric and oratory.

In his arsenal there are winged sandals and a wide-brimmed hat with small wings, facilitating the rapid movements of the patron of trade. And to convey the will of the gods to mortals, he uses a golden scepter that can induce sleep.

Hestia - goddess of the hearth

Zeus's sister, the goddess of home and hospitality, Hestia, was depicted as a modest middle-aged woman in simple clothes and with a hood thrown over her head. A flame or a bowl with fire always appears next to her; less often, Hestia holds a staff in her hands.

In mythology, this character was distinguished by the most balanced and calm disposition. The goddess did not enter into scandals and quarrels, for which she was given the honor of keeping the fire in the sacred hearth of the gods. But also in the land of Greece, the hearth occupied a central place in the homes of mortals: food was prepared on it, people warmed themselves in front of it, and on days of celebration, sacrifices were made.

Hephaestus - god of blacksmithing (fire)

Hephaestus is an atypical representative of the Olympic elite: he works tirelessly and also has a physical disability - lameness. God of fire, builder, master, and patron of the blacksmith's craft, he is depicted as a strong man wielding tongs and a hammer. Hephaestus is wearing work clothes and a hat.

On antique vases, there is also another image of God, comic or, conversely, triumphant. On it, the patron of blacksmiths appears drunk with wine and sitting on a donkey while ascending Olympus. This image is associated with the myth according to which the baby Hephaestus was thrown from the mountain of the gods into the ocean because he was weak and had congenital lameness.

With his talent and cunning, the now mature Hephaestus regained his place on Olympus, taking revenge on his mother for her expulsion with the help of the iron throne given to her, which bound Hera with invisible fetters.

Hymen - god of marriage

Along with Hera, the god Hymen, the son of Dionysus and Aphrodite, also patronized family ties. When depicting him, they use the image of a charming young man carrying a lit torch, which ignites the fire of true love.

Garlands of flowers are hung across his neck, also symbolizing a happy married life. Sometimes a lush flowering vine is in the hand of a god. Hymen's face is stern and confident, which indicates the seriousness of the spouses' intentions, and not a casual love affair.

In addition, Hymen also personifies the marriage song. Over time, his name was somewhat transformed, shortened to "hymn," and today it represents any solemn song.

Hypnos - god of sleep

In the myths of Ancient Greece, Sleep and Death were siblings, relentlessly following each other. Hypnos patronized sleep and was depicted as a beautiful young man with wings, soaring above the world with a horn in his hands. From this horn, a magical sleeping pill nectar poured out on mortals, and they plunged into the oblivion of a night's sleep and saw dreams.

4

Literature and Philosophy

The world of ancient Greek culture is completely special. The Greeks were perhaps the first people who tried to describe themselves. They had enormous curiosity about themselves and the world, which is why we know so much about them.

This research interest of the Greeks, the ability to observe and understand people, was inherited by European civilization. The ancient Greeks left their mark in all areas of culture and science. Suffice it to remember that Greek writing underlies most modern alphabets.

Ancient Greek science. Philosophy

In the VI century. BC. The famous mathematician Pythagoras said: "I am not a sage, I am only a lover of wisdom (in Greek, "philosopher"). Greek philosophy was born from the desire to bring together all known information about the world around us and understand it. Greek myths helped people navigate the world, explaining in their way how it works but did not answer the question of why the world works this way. Philosophy, which grew out of mythology, aimed to answer the question:

"Why?" In search of truth, philosophers moved from describing the world around us to analyzing it, from concrete images and feelings to abstract concepts.

The first philosophers, including those numbered among the seven sages, sought the fundamental principle of the world - that from which it was created, its beginning. For Thales it was water, for Anaximenes it was air, for Heraclitus it was fire (either flaming or dying out). Heraclitus said: "Everything flows, everything changes. You cannot step into the same river twice." The search for the fundamental principle led Pericles' friend Anaxagoras, and then Democritus, to divide all substances in nature into the smallest particles. Democritus called them atoms and believed that even the gods were made of them.

Later, Greek philosophers began to think more not about the nature of things, but about the nature of man: his character, passions, deceitful and righteous actions. Sophists undertook to teach anyone how to build logical reasoning and prove any idea that appeared. Respectable Greeks were extremely outraged by this "trade in wisdom."

Many Athenians of the 4th century were "troublemakers." BC. They considered Socrates, who, through difficult questions, forced people to think about their behavior, about the laws of good. As a result, the court sentenced the philosopher to death. Socrates' faithful student Plato, thanks to whom we know about the life of Socrates (the sage himself did not keep notes, believing that they kill the ever-changing thought), created his philosophical system. He believed that the world can only be known by reason since all objects are just shadows, a reflection of the ideas of objects that exist in a special world of ideas. He also developed a picture of an ideal state in which all residents were divided into philosophers, guards, and workers.

Democritus

Plato organized a philosophical school in the grove of the hero Academus near Athens - the Academy. One of the students in this school was Aristotle, the greatest philosopher of antiquity. Later, he also opened his school - in the grove of Apollo Lyceum, from whose name the modern word "lyceum" comes.

Although the names of modern sciences - mathematics, biology, history, geography, and others - come from Greek words, in Ancient Greece itself they were not yet separated from each other, as they are today. Ancient scientists, as a rule, made discoveries in many areas at once. Philosophy remained the basis of the sciences. The philosopher Pythagoras compiled a multiplication table and proved the famous theorem, the philosopher Anaxagoras considered the stars and the Sun to be red-hot spherical bodies, and in Plato's philosophical Academy there was an inscription: "Let no one who does not know geometry enter here."

Finally, in the 4th century. BC. Aristotle attempted to generalize and systematize in strict sequence the knowledge accumulated by the Greeks in the fields of biology, physics, rhetoric, history, astronomy, logic, etc. He wrote several dozen treatises, including "On the Movement of Animals", "Mechanics", "On the Directions and Names of the Winds", and "On the Soul". It was Aristotle who substantiated many of the concepts and approaches that modern sciences currently rely on.

The world of ancient Greek culture is completely special. The Greeks were perhaps the first people who tried to describe themselves. They had enormous curiosity about themselves and the world, which is why we know so much about them.

This research interest of the Greeks, the ability to observe and understand people, was inherited by European civilization. The ancient Greeks left their mark in all areas of culture and science. Suffice it to remember that Greek writing underlies most modern alphabets.

Ancient Greek science. Philosophy

In the VI century. BC. The famous mathematician Pythagoras said: "I am not a sage, I am only a lover of wisdom (in Greek, "philosopher"). Greek philosophy was born from the desire to bring together all known information about the world around us and understand it. Greek myths helped people navigate the world, explaining in their way how it works but did not answer the question of why the world works this way. Philosophy, which grew out of mythology, aimed to answer the question: "Why?" In search of truth, philosophers moved from describing the world around us to analyzing it, from concrete images and feelings to abstract concepts.

The first philosophers, including those numbered among the seven sages, sought the fundamental principle of the world - that from which it was created, its beginning. For Thales it was water, for Anaximenes it was air, for Heraclitus it was fire (either flaming or dying out). Heraclitus said: "Everything flows, everything changes. You cannot step into the same river twice." The search for the fundamental principle led Pericles' friend Anaxagoras, and then Democritus, to the idea of dividing all substances in nature into the smallest particles. Democritus called them atoms and believed that even the gods were made of them.

Later, Greek philosophers began to think more not about the nature of things, but about the nature of man: his character, passions, deceitful and righteous actions. Sophists appeared who undertook to teach any person how to build logical reasoning and prove any idea. Respectable Greeks were extremely outraged by this "trade in wisdom."

Many Athenians of the 4th century were "troublemakers." BC. They considered Socrates, who, through difficult questions, forced people to think about their behavior, about the laws of good. As a result, the court sentenced the philosopher to death. Socrates' faithful student Plato, thanks to whom we know about the life of Socrates (the sage himself did not keep notes, believing that they kill the ever-changing thought), created his philosophical system. He believed that the world can only be known by reason since all objects in it are just shadows, a reflection of the ideas of objects that exist in a special world of ideas. He also developed a picture of an ideal state in which all residents were divided into philosophers, guards, and workers

Plato organized a philosophical school in the grove of the hero Academus near Athens - the Academy. One of the students in this school was Aristotle, the greatest philosopher of antiquity. Later, he also opened his school - in the grove of Apollo Lyceum, from whose name the modern word "lyceum" comes.

Although the names of modern sciences - mathematics, biology, history, geography, and others - come from Greek words, in Ancient Greece itself they were not yet separated from each other, as they are today. Ancient scientists, as a rule, made discoveries in many areas at once. Philosophy remained the basis of the sciences. The philosopher Pythagoras compiled a multiplication table and proved the famous theorem, the philosopher Anaxagoras considered the stars and the Sun to be red-hot spherical bodies, and in Plato's philosophical Academy there was an inscription: "Let no one who does not know geometry enter here."

Finally, in the 4th century. BC. Aristotle attempted to generalize and systematize in strict sequence the knowledge accumulated by the Greeks in the fields of biology, physics, rhetoric, history, astronomy, logic, etc. He wrote several dozen treatises, including "On the Movement of Animals",

"Mechanics", "On the Directions and Names of the Winds", and "On the Soul". It was Aristotle who substantiated many of the concepts and approaches that modern sciences currently rely on.

Literature

The origins of ancient Greek literature are the epic works of the 8th–7th centuries. - Homer's great poems "Iliad" and "Odyssey" and Hesiod's work "Works and Days". A legend has been preserved about the competition between Homer and Hesiod and the award of victory to Hesiod because he glorified peaceful labor, not war. During the archaic period in Greece, a different kind of poetry began to flourish. Aristocrats worshiped beauty and wanted to listen to lyrical poetry intended for a small circle of connoisseurs.

The most famous author of love poems was the poet Sappho. Also, poets of those times composed solemn chants for festive choirs, to glorify the winners of various competitions. Among them, Pindar and Arion became famous and wrote the first dithyramb - a hymn to Dionysus. With the emergence of the theater, new poetic genres appeared - tragedy and comedy, new authors, and new artistic ideas.

Prose works were created by historians - Herodotus, Thucydides, and Xenophon. History itself in ancient times was considered an artistic narrative. Also, the speeches of Athenian orators, primarily Demosthenes, became examples of artistic prose. The authors of philosophical works, Plato and Aristotle, attached great importance to literary decoration and the language of their works.

The ancient Greeks themselves were the first to study their literature. They also introduced the word "philology" (from the Greek words

"Philo" - "to love", and "logos" - "thought", "word"). However, they attributed to philology a love for all kinds of academic pursuits. The first philologist in the modern sense of the word was Aristotle. He created an essay on the laws of literary creativity - "Poetics" (it has not reached our days in full).

Architecture

In the art of the Greeks in the V–IV centuries. BC. reflected the customs, views, and tastes of the free Hellenes. This time differs from previous periods of Greek art in such completeness and perfection that it was called classical - exemplary.

Architecture is defined as a "style-forming art": it sets the rhythm, image, size, line, and even color of other types - sculpture, painting, decorative and applied arts.

The urban planning of Greek classics was based on the architectural order. During this period there were two of them - the strict and majestic Doric and the light, graceful Ionic. During the Hellenistic period, the refined and luxurious Corinthian style began to spread. The most common public buildings in Greece were temples. Depending on the number of columns, they were divided into several types. The solemn and elegant appearance of the temple was given by the pediment with sculptures and reliefs, the upper parts of the outer walls, and porticoes with columns, permeated with air and light. The columns created a gradual transition from space to temple.

The Greeks believed that the temples of the Olympian gods, who brought order to the world, should be built in the same harmonious and orderly manner.

Inside the temple there was a statue of the god whose home this temple was considered, sacred objects and treasures, and often the city treasury was kept here. The Greek temple, unlike the Christian church, was intended for external inspection by people; all its beauty was on the outside, and not on the inside.

Greek architects not only masterfully created individual buildings. Their achievement was the development of the idea of a regular city, that is, the construction of cities according to a premeditated, reasonable plan. It was invented by Hippodamus of Miletus. Although his proposals were suitable for cities in a new location (for example, Piraeus was built according to his plan), in ancient cities like Athens they also tried to architecturally highlight the Acropolis and Agora, and build theaters and stadiums in certain places.

The concept of an architectural ensemble appeared - the unity and artistic connection of buildings and sculptures built nearby, "inscribed" in the landscape. An example of such an ensemble was the Athenian Acropolis, rebuilt under Pericles under the leadership of Phidias. The architectural ensemble of the Acropolis included the Propylaea (an elegant entrance), the Pinakothek (a place for storing paintings), the temple of the goddess Nike Apteros (Wingless), the Erechtheion and the most famous surviving ancient Greek structure - the Parthenon.

The Temple of Athena stood not in the center of the Acropolis, but on the side, at the very top. When creating it, the architects Iktin and Kallikrates decided not to cramp or level the upper platform of the rock. This created the feeling that the temple was growing out of nature itself and at the same time triumphing over its stone chaos. Spectators compared the Parthenon to a bird ready to take flight.

Classical Greek architecture was proportionate to man. It did not suppress with its power and inaccessibility, like the Egyptian or Persian, but, as it were, raised a person to the level of a hero. The Greeks figuratively said that "one must grow to the steps of the Parthenon."

The architects of the Parthenon took into account the characteristics of the human eye, which distorts the proportions of objects.

Therefore, they made the middle of the steps, columns, and especially the cornice a little thicker, so that they would not appear to sag under the weight, and the corner columns were slightly thickened and placed closer to the neighboring ones because an object in space looks thinner than it is. Thus, Greek architecture, even when creating temples to the gods, was focused on human perception. She fully embodied the words of the philosopher Protagoras: "Man is the measure of all things."

The spirit of freedom, harmony, and human proportionality was inherited from the Greek classics by all subsequent European architecture.

II

Pillars of Greek Thought and Culture

5

Philosophy and the Pursuit of Wisdom

The Presocratic thinkers were early Greek philosophers who laid the foundation for Western philosophy and science. They were primarily concerned with understanding the nature of the universe and the fundamental principles that govern it. Thales, Anaximander, and Anaximenes, for example, sought to identify the basic substance from which everything is derived, while Heraclitus and Parmenides explored the nature of change and permanence. Their inquiries into the cosmos and the underlying principles of reality set the stage for the development of metaphysics, epistemology, and natural philosophy, shaping the way we approach questions about the universe to this day.

Presocratic Thinkers and Questions about the Universe

The history of philosophy begins in the pre-Sacratic period. It is from this moment that the countdown of all philosophy begins. Chronological judgments do not belong to the historical continuum as such but originate in the minds of historical scientists who form all sorts of reconstructions of the historical process, highlighting in it important structures and main events, in the light of which other events deserve this or that meaning.

Such meaningful structures are called paradigms. Based on all this, history is a paradigm shift. The very first paradigm is ancient pre-Socratic philosophy.

Determining the beginning of a process, much less the beginning of a new scientific discipline is quite difficult. Any historical reconstruction faces a similar problem. One might assume that the beginning is where they begin to recreate the historical process, but in reality, everything is much more complicated. The beginning of the history of any phenomenon depends entirely on our understanding of this phenomenon. Moreover, it is also important to give some definition to this process.

The search for the beginning of philosophy and any other science will not be successful if there is not at least the slightest idea of what philosophy is. Thus, speaking about the beginning of the countdown, it is first necessary to turn to the researcher himself, who is engaged in the reconstruction of a historical phenomenon, having previously given himself an account of what this phenomenon is.

The first who began to explore the question of the beginning of philosophy was Aristotle. Having supported his knowledge and principles with sufficient material and theoretical base, he turned to the experience of his predecessors and attempted to interpret their views from a historical and philosophical point of view. Not a single one of his works is complete without quoting his predecessors. It is worth noting that he vehemently criticized some, and agreed with others.

However, it is important to say that his criticism was justified and supported by his knowledge. He was guided by his doctrine of the four causes of everything:

1. Material reason. What is it from?
2. Formal reason. What.
3. Driving reason. That's where the movement comes from.
4. Target reason. That's why.

Aristotle believed that almost all the first philosophers believed that the beginning of everything was material principles. In other words, what things are made of, what they come from, and what they turn into after death, while it is important that the essence, although it remains, can change in its manifestations.

Aristotle calls such an entity physics, which translated means nature or nature. Aristotle sees Thales as the origin of such philosophy. The philosophical direction that corresponds to this type of philosophy is called physiology by Aristotle, and thinkers belonging to this direction are called physiologists.

Aristotle's historical and philosophical excursions took on an academic character and became quite authoritarian during other eras, which had an important impact on the order of presentation of philosophical thought in the future.

Early Greek philosophy received the name pre-Socratic thanks to the German historian of philosophy of the 19th century. E. Zeller. From the German Vorsokratiker. It is noteworthy that the part of the word vor, which in Russian means before, can be explained in several meanings. Understanding in the literal sense means that before indicates the chronological component and indicates the period that was before Socrates, and also names all the representatives of this pre-Socratic era.

But upon deeper study of this topic, it turns out that many of those who were considered pre-Socratics were similar in age or even younger than Socrates himself. This meant that Socrates was definitely a key figure in the development and establishment of philosophical thought, and his place was somewhere between before and after.

The second reason for doubting an unambiguous understanding of the concept is that some thinkers stand out as a separate group also because their understanding of philosophy differed from Socratic ideas. Their type of philosophizing was not similar to the type of philosophizing of Socrates; they explored other problems and set themselves other goals.

This was the case, the sophists were rather contemporaries of Socrates, but it is important to note that they were also his teachers, and a little later they became his opponents because they built their views rather on the ideas of early philosophers. The Sophists were closer to the views of Parmenides, Heraclitus, and Zeno of Elea, but the radical ideas of Socrates were alien to them.

Philosophical position of the Presocratics

The texts that have come down to us help to establish the direction of the ideas of the Pre-Socratics. Fragments and contemporary evidence suggest that the most important question for the early Greek philosophers was the question of the beginning of the unity of everything. The daily observations of thinkers led them to think that nothing in the world lasts forever, but this does not cause the world to perish. Every day various changes occur in the environment, something dies, something is born again, but these constant changes do not lead to the disappearance of the world. Moreover, every person constantly observes many things and events around him, but at the same time, the world remains integral.

This means, as the Pre-Socratics believed, there must be some kind of force that has an invisible effect aimed at preserving the whole, and, being many, it continues to exist as a single world, and anything in this world exists as a single one, and from here it becomes clear that the force or power that helps maintain this unity and allows it to be so is the thing itself in this world itself. Otherwise, nothing can exist.

Early thinkers put forward many hypotheses about what this force could be and who could fill this necessary role. According to pre-Socratic philosophical teachings and the idea that they put forward, such a unifying role could be played by water, air, fire, and much more.

Pre-Socratics are scientists and thinkers who lived in the 6th - beginning of the century. IV century BC, their main occupation was the study of nature in the sense of physis, in other words, fusiology, the key issue of their study was the principle of the beginning of the unity of the whole world.

Some scientists believe that the Sophists, who also studied nature during this period, can also be classified as Pre-Socratics. However, some deny this position because the sophists based their interests in a different area than the fusiologists.

Socrates, Plato, and the Development of Idealism

In the 5th - 4th centuries BC. Socrates and Plato spoke out against slave-owning democracy, against natural science and materialism, continuing the line of the Pythagoreans in politics and philosophy. The crisis of Athenian democracy, which worsened after the defeat in the Peloponnesian War, intensified the forces of reaction. Socrates lived and preached at a time when democratic Athens led a powerful maritime alliance of states against the Peloponnesian League, led by aristocratic Sparta.

Being an Athenian citizen, Socrates, organized a circle of aristocrats around himself and made it the center of the struggle against Athenian democracy. Plato was also a member of this circle. Socrates widely disseminated his reactionary views. His doubt ("I know that I know nothing"), leading (469 - 399 BC) supposedly to self-knowledge ("Know thyself"), was not abstract philosophizing, but a thoughtful form of "justification" and proclamation of political views.

The religious-idealistic ethics of Socrates were aimed at instilling fear of God and humility in the Athenians and had the goal of turning ordinary citizens into obedient instruments of "noble masters." Socrates sought to undermine scientific knowledge of nature as a supposedly godless endeavor and actively fought against ancient Greek science, materialism, and atheism. In contrast to the materialists who called for "listening to nature" (Heraclitus), Socrates referred to his "inner voice" ("demon" of Socrates). In contrast to the determinism of materialists who sought to understand the causes of phenomena occurring in the world, Socrates developed teleological views, according to which the will of the gods predetermined the goals for each of the phenomena.

Socrates was also one of the founders of philosophical dialectics. Karl Marx called Socrates "the personification of philosophy," and "philosophy embodied" (see K. Marx and F. Engels, Works, 2nd ed., vol. 1, p. 99). Considering ancient natural philosophy unsatisfactory, Socrates turned to the analysis of human consciousness and thinking. Gravitating toward objective idealism, he was still far from hypostatizing general concepts in the form of independent entities. This is how Aristotle portrays him, who attributes to Socrates the inductive doctrine of the transition from fluid reality to general concepts, as well as the doctrine of the definition of concepts, which for the first time makes it possible to know the essence of each thing. Recognition of the action of generic essences in the surrounding reality was transformed by Socrates into a doctrine of general and universal reason or individual god-minds.

In ethics, the main thesis of Socrates was that virtue is knowledge, or wisdom, that he who knows good necessarily acts in a good way, and he who acts in evil either does not know what good is or does evil for the final triumph of good. In Socrates' understanding, there can be no contradiction between reason and behavior.

After the restoration of democracy in Athens, Socrates was executed (he took hemlock poison), as the official accusation stated, for the introduction of new deities and for corrupting youth in a new spirit. After the death of Socrates, his student Plato took over the baton of the development of idealism.

The activities of Plato, the enemy of slave-holding democracy, unfolded after the victory of the combined forces of Sparta and its Peloponnesian allies, supported financially by Persia, over democratic Athens, when the military defeats of Athens greatly aggravated the class struggle in Ancient Greece. Having fled from Athens after the execution of Socrates, Plato maintained contact with the Pythagoreans and everywhere defended the interests of the aristocratic nobility of Syracuse (Sicily). The philosophical school founded by Plato in Athens - the "Academy" - was the main center of ancient idealism in its reactionary struggle against science. Not

Plato, being able to refute the arguments of materialists and suppress (427 - 347 BC) the growing influence of materialism, Plato spoke with hatred of Democritus and his followers as atheists, accused them of spreading "ungodly" thoughts, and attributed to them all sorts of fables. Plato reworked the idealism of Socrates into a system of objective idealism, according to which the world of eternal and unchanging ideas forms "true being," and changeable and transitory sensory things constitute only shadows of the world of ideas. True knowledge, Plato said, developing the mysticism of the Pythagoreans and Socrates, is the memories of the immortal soul about the ideas that it contemplated before entering a mortal body.

Plato's philosophy is not systematically presented in his works, as a result Plato's system has to be reconstructed. Its most important part is the doctrine of three main ontological substances (triad): "one", "mind" and "soul"; adjacent to it is the doctrine of "cosmos". The basis of all being, according to Plato, is the "one", which in itself is devoid of any characteristics, has no parts, i.e. neither beginning nor end, does not occupy any space, cannot move, since change is necessary for movement, i.e. plurality; signs of identity, difference, similarity, etc. do not apply to it. Nothing can be said about it at all; it is above all being, sensation, and thinking. This source hides not only the "ideas" or "eidos" of things (i.e., their substantial spiritual prototypes and principles to which Plato attributes timeless reality) but also the things themselves, and their formation.

The second substance - "mind" (nous) is, according to Plato, the existential-light generation of the "single" - "good". The mind is of a pure and unmixed nature; Plato carefully distinguishes it from everything material, substantial, and becoming: "mind" is intuitive and its subject has the essence of things, but not their becoming. Finally, the dialectical concept of "mind" culminates in the cosmological concept. "Mind" is a mental generic generalization of all living beings, a living being, or life itself, given in the utmost generality, orderliness, perfection, and beauty. This "mind" is embodied in the "cosmos," namely in the regular and eternal movement of the sky.

The third substance - the "world soul" - unites Plato's "mind" and the physical world. Receiving the laws of its movement from the "mind," the "soul" differs from it in its eternal mobility; this is the principle of self-propulsion. "Mind" is incorporeal and immortal; The "soul" unites it with the physical world with something beautiful, proportional, and harmonious, being itself immortal, and also involved in truth and eternal ideas. The individual soul is the image and outflow of the "world soul". Plato spoke about immortality, or rather, about the eternal emergence of the body along with the "soul." The death of a body is its transition to another state.

"Ideas" are the ultimate generalization, the meaning, the semantic essence of things, and the very principle of their comprehension. They have not only a logical but also a certain artistic structure; they are characterized by their own, ideal matter, the design of which makes it possible to understand them aesthetically. The beautiful also exists in the ideal world, it is such an embodiment of an idea that is the limit and semantic anticipation of all its possible partial embodiments; it is a kind of organism of an idea, or, more precisely, an idea as an organism. Further dialectical development of the prototype leads to the mind, soul, and body of the "cosmos", which for the first time creates beauty in its final form. "Cosmos", which perfectly reproduces the eternal prototype or model ("paradigm"), is the most beautiful. Related to this is Plato's doctrine of cosmic proportions.

Matter for Plato is only the principle of the partial functioning of an idea, its reduction, diminution, and darkening, as it were, the "successor" and "nurse" of ideas. In itself, it is formless, it is neither earth, nor water, nor air, nor any physical element at all; Matter is not a being, but a being is only an idea. Plato sharply criticized the separation of ideas and things and formulated the very arguments that Aristotle later directed against Plato's supposed dualism. True being for Plato is an ideal being, which exists in itself, and is only "present" in matter. Matter first receives its existence from imitating it, joining it, or "participating" in it.

In the last years of his life, Plato reworked the doctrine of ideas in the spirit of Pythagoreanism, now seeing their source in "ideal numbers," which played an exceptional role in the development of Neoplatonism. The basis of Plato's theory of knowledge is the delight of love for the idea, so that delight and knowledge turned out to be an inseparable whole, and Plato in a vivid artistic form depicted the ascent from bodily love to love in the realm of souls, and from the latter to the realm of pure ideas. He understood this synthesis of love ("eros") and knowledge as a special kind of frenzy and ecstasy, erotic enthusiasm. In mythological form, this knowledge was interpreted by Plato as the recollection of souls about their heavenly homeland, where they directly perceived every idea.

For Plato, the main science that defines all others is dialectics - the method of dividing the one into the many, reducing the many to the one, and structurally representing the whole as a single multiplicity. Dialectics, entering the realm of confused things, dismembers them so that each thing receives its meaning, its idea. This meaning, or idea of a thing, is taken as the principle of the thing, as its "hypothesis," the law ("nomos"), which in Plato leads from scattered sensuality to an ordered idea and back; This is exactly how Plato understands logos. Dialectics is therefore the establishment of mental foundations for things, a kind of objective a priori categories or forms of meaning. These logos - idea - hypothesis - -foundation is also interpreted as the limit ("goal") of sensory formation. Such a universal goal is good in the Republic, Philebus, Gorgias, or Beauty in the Symposium. This limit of the formation of a thing contains in a compressed form the entire formation of a thing and is, as it were, its plan, its structure. In this regard, dialectics in Plato is a doctrine of indivisible wholes; as such it is at once discursive and intuitive; making all kinds of logical divisions, she knows how to merge everything. A dialectician, according to Plato, has a "total vision" of the sciences, and "sees everything at once."

The individual soul has three abilities: mental, volitional, and affective - with the primacy of the first of them. In ethics, this corresponds to three virtues - wisdom, courage, and an enlightened state of effect, which are combined into one integral virtue representing their balance - "justice".

Plato carried out the same triple division in politics, in the theory of three classes: philosophers, who, based on the contemplation of ideas, govern the entire state; soldiers, whose main goal is to protect the state from internal and external enemies, and workers, i.e. peasants and artisans who support the state financially, providing it with vital resources. Plato identified three main forms of government - monarchy, aristocracy, and democracy.

Each of them, in turn, is divided into two forms. Monarchy can be legal (king) or violent (tyrant); aristocracy can be the dominion of the best or the worst (oligarchy); democracy can be legal or lawless, violent. Plato sharply criticized all six forms of state power, putting forward a utopian ideal of state and social structure. According to Plato, kings should philosophize, and philosophers should reign, and only a few contemplatives of truth can be such. Having developed a detailed theory of societies. and the personal education of philosophers and warriors, Plato did not classify her as a "worker." Plato preached the abolition of private property, the community of wives and children, state regulation of marriage, and the public education of children who should not know their parents. K. Marx characterized Plato's utopia in The Republic as "… the Athenian idealization of the Egyptian caste system" (K. Marx and F. Engels, Works, 2nd ed., vol. 23, p. 379).

In Plato's aesthetics, beauty is understood as the absolute interpenetration of body, soul, and mind, the fusion of idea and matter, rationality, and pleasure, and the principle of this fusion is the measure. In Plato knowledge is not separated from love, and love is not separated from beauty ("Symposium", "Phaedrus"). Everything beautiful, that is, is visible and audible, externally or bodily, it is animated by its inner life and contains one meaning or another. Such beauty turned out to be the ruler and, in general, the source of life for all living things in Plato.

The beauty of life and real existence for Plato is higher than the beauty of art. Being and life are an imitation of eternal ideas, and art is an imitation of being and life, i.e. imitation. Therefore, Plato expelled Homer (although he placed him above all the poets of Greece) from his ideal state, since it is the creativity of life, and not of fiction, even beautiful ones. Plato expelled sad, softening, or table music from his state, leaving only military or generally courageous and peacefully active music. Good manners and decency are a necessary condition for beauty.

Without rejecting the gods of traditional mythology, Plato demanded their philosophical cleansing of everything coarse, immoral, and fantastic. He considered it unacceptable for susceptible children to become familiar with most myths. Myth, according to Plato, is a symbol; in mythological form, he set out the periods and ages of the cosmos, the cosmic movement of gods and souls in general, etc.

Hellenistic Philosophy and its Impact on Later Civilizations

Hellenistic philosophy is the last period in the development of the philosophy of Ancient Greece, which began with the conquests of Alexander the Great in the 6th and 3rd centuries. BC. and ended already in the 6th century. AD with the closure of Plato's last school. At this time, four philosophical schools were formed in Athens: the Academy, the Lyceum, the Garden, and the Stoa. Hellenic philosophy was aimed at understanding and improving existence. The focus of the study was society and the individual.

One of the features of Hellenistic philosophy is its appeal to ethical issues. The main task of philosophy was to find ways to improve human life and achieve great benefits.

Directions and representatives

Cynics

The direction was based on simplification. Man, according to the Kinians, must give up luxury and wealth and become closer to nature. Any power over a person was also rejected. The highest good is freedom.

The most famous philosophers of this movement are Antisthenes and his student Diogenes, who became famous for their judgments and way of life. According to legend, the philosopher lived in a barrel, did not recognize rulers and the state, and also denied state borders.

Skeptics

The main principle of skepticism is that the world is changeable, every concept and object has two sides. Therefore, no statement can be considered true. In this regard, the real happiness of a person lies in serenity and equanimity. A prominent representative of this trend was Pyrrho. Among other things, he called for an ascetic lifestyle.

Epicurus

The movement got its name from its founder, the philosopher Epicurus. The main thesis of Epicureanism is a true sensation. Through sensations a person comes to spiritual pleasure. A true understanding of spiritual pleasure can only be gained by a person who consciously avoids negative emotions, develops fortitude, and strives for pleasure. Only by rejecting all worries can a person achieve harmony.

Stoics

Three movements were included in Stoicism - logic, ethics, and physics. The teaching was based on ethical principles. A person must be resistant to temptation and control his feelings with the help of reason. The main good is virtue.

The followers of the teaching were such philosophers as Zeno of Elea, Seneca, Cicero, and Marcus Aurelius.

Neoplatonists

One of the features of the current is the creation of a hierarchy of human society, at the top of which is the superintelligent divine principle. Among people, followers of Neoplatonism distinguished between simple and wise people. They differed about the material and spiritual worlds. The simple are characterized by a physical principle, while the sages are characterized by a moral and metaphysical principle.

One of the characteristics of Neoplatonism is the desire for a synthesis of various teachings: from nascent Christianity to Eastern mythology.

The founder of the school was Plato's student Plotinus. It is noteworthy that Neoplatonism became a transitional link between antiquity and theism.

```
Hellenistic philosophy refers to the period of ancient Greek
philosophy that occurred after the death of Alexander the
Great in 323 BCE. This period is characterized by a shift in
philosophical focus from metaphysical and epistemological
```

concerns to more practical issues related to human life in society. The impact of Hellenistic philosophy can be seen in later civilizations such as Rome, and it played a significant role in shaping Western philosophy.

6

Science and Mathematics: Seeking Knowledge of the World

Mathematics is one of the oldest, most important, and most complex components of human culture. The history of mathematics is connected with the history of other sciences in thousands of threads. Popular wisdom says that it is impossible to understand the true meaning of the present and future goals if you do not know and appreciate the past. Life did not stand still. With the development of humanity, the need arises to transmit news to each other, write, and count.

Mathematics Knowledge

This is how mathematics gradually emerged in the distant past. The ancient Greeks were an amazingly talented people from whom there is much to learn. At that time, Greece consisted of many small states. Every time an important state issue had to be resolved, the townspeople gathered in the square, discussed it, argued, and then voted. They were good debaters. According to legend, at that time there was a statement: "Truth is born in a dispute!" The Greeks were distinguished by their hard work and courage. Among them were excellent builders, sailors, merchants, and artists.

They made a great contribution to the development of culture and science, especially mathematics. History knows that the mathematicians of ancient Greece were the greatest mathematicians in the distant past and the problems they compiled are still interesting today. A very large part of our modern school mathematics course, especially geometry, was known to the ancient Greeks. A teacher will never begin to present a new topic, not to mention a new section of mathematics, without an introductory historical part that arouses the interest and attention of the students. Lessons involving historical material leave no one indifferent. How, when introducing students to the basic concepts of 7th-grade geometry, can you not talk about Greek mathematics?.. How when studying the topic "Area" 8th grade. cannot explain the measurement of areas in Ancient Greece (solving ancient problems). It is here that the connection between historical information and the material of the topic under consideration is established. The history of mathematics acts as a means of activating the cognitive activity of students. This is the basis of educational activities for the following reasons:

1. Interest contributes to the formation of deep and lasting knowledge.
2. Develops and improves the quality of mental activity, and activity in learning, favors the formation of abilities.
3. Creates a more favorable emotional background for the flow of all mental processes.

An excursion into history can be accompanied by pictures, slides, and presentations. Since its inception as a science and much earlier, mathematics has been closely connected not only with civilization, and with practice, but also with the entire human culture - with the whole world. Both mathematical theories and methods were discovered and created by specific individuals, mathematicians, whose life and fate, interesting and rich, instructive and sometimes tragic, are inseparable from the historical era in which they worked.

Mathematics Scientists of Greece

Let's talk about Pythagoras, after whom a theorem that everyone knows is named. The scientist Pythagoras lived in Ancient Greece (he was born around 580 BC and died in 500 BC). Little is known about the life of this scientist, but several legends are associated with his name. They say that he traveled a lot, was in India, Egypt, and Babylon, and studied ancient culture and scientific achievements of different countries. Returning to his homeland, Pythagoras organized a circle of youth from representatives of the aristocracy. They were accepted into the circle with great ceremonies after long trials. Each entrant renounced his property and swore an oath to keep the founder's teachings secret. Thus, in the south of Italy, which was then a Greek colony, the so-called Pythagorean school arose.

The Pythagoreans studied mathematics, philosophy, and natural sciences. They made many important discoveries in arithmetic and geometry. There was a decree at school according to which the authorship of all mathematical works was attributed to Pythagoras. Pythagoras was killed in a street battle during a popular uprising. After his death, the students surrounded the name of their teacher with many legends, so it is impossible to establish the truth about Pythagoras. The Pythagorean theorem has a rich history. It turns out that long before Pythagoras it was known to the Egyptians, Babylonians, Chinese, and Indians. The proof of Pythagoras himself has not reached us. There are currently over 100 pieces of evidence. One of them may belong to Pythagoras and his students.

Archimedes is the pinnacle of scientific thought in the ancient world. Archimedes was born in 287 BC in the Greek city of Syracuse, where he lived almost his entire life. His father was Phidias, the court astronomer of the ruler of the city of Heron. Archimedes studied in Alexandria, where the rulers of Egypt, the Ptolemies, gathered the best Greek scientists and thinkers and also founded the world's largest library. Archimedes' main works concerned various practical applications of mathematics, physics, hydrostatics, and mechanics. In his work "Parabolas of Quadrature," Archimedes substantiated the method for calculating the area of a parabolic segment, and he did this two thousand years before the discovery of integral calculus. In his work "On the Measurement of a Circle," Archimedes first calculated the number "pi" - the ratio of the circumference of a circle to its diameter - and proved that it is the same for any circle. Archimedes, died when the Romans captured his hometown of Syracuse at the time when a Roman soldier arrived. According to legend, Archimedes was passionate about solving a geometric problem, the drawing of which was made in sand. The soldier who killed Archimedes either did not know about the commander's order to save Archimedes' life or did not recognize Archimedes. In our time, the name Archimedes is associated mainly with his remarkable mathematical works, but in antiquity, he also became famous as the inventor of various kinds of mechanical devices and tools, as reported by authors who lived in a later era. It is believed that Archimedes was the inventor of the so-called. the Archimedean screw, which served to lift water to the fields and was the prototype of ship and air propellers.

Euclid. The ancient Greek scientist Euclid wrote works on mechanics, optics, and music. His achievements in astronomy are also known. Several theorems and new proofs are also attributed to Euclid

Of the works of Euclid that have come down to us, the most famous are the Elements, consisting of 15 books. The 1st book formulates the initial provisions of geometry and also contains the fundamental theorems of planimetry, including the theorem on the sum of the angles of a triangle and the Pythagorean theorem. When constructing regular polygons, this name of Euclid again sounds. Book XIII of "Principles" is dedicated to the Platonic solids - regular polyhedra, the beauty of which we admire in stereometry lessons. Considering the issues of differential and integral calculus in analysis lessons, we say that the ideas underlying them by Newton and Leibniz in the 17th century are rooted in the method of exhaustion, discovered by Euclid and Archimedes.

Thales of Miletus (c.625 - c.547 BC) ancient Greek scientist and statesman, the first of the seven sages. During his travels, he visited Egypt, where he became acquainted with astronomy and geometry. The legend says that Thales amazed the Egyptian king Amasis by measuring the height of one of the pyramids by the size of the shadow it cast. Problem. Measure the height of the pyramid by the shadow it casts. (Dimensions are given in elbows; 1 elbow = 7 palms = 466 mm.)

The founder and founder of Greek philosophy and science. It is believed that Thales was the first to prove several geometric theorems, namely:

- Vertical angles are equal;
- Triangles with one equal side and equal adjacent angles are congruent;
- The angles at the base of an isosceles triangle are equal;
- Diameter divides the circle in half;
- An angle inscribed in a semicircle will always be right.

Thales determined the height of an object by its shadow, and the distance to ships, using the likeness of triangles.

He made several discoveries in the field of astronomy, established the time of the equinoxes and solstices, and determined the length of the year. Thales was ranked among the group of "seven wise men."

Eratosthenes of Cyrene (c. 276 - 194 BC) is a versatile scientist: mathematician, astronomer, geographer, historian, and philologist. He became famous for his invention of the "Sieve of Eratosthenes". In his work "The Sieve," Eratosthenes created an original method for "sifting out" prime numbers. In the sequence of natural numbers, cross out 1. Number 2 is prime. Let's cross out all the numbers that are multiples of 2. The number 3, the first of the uncrossed ones, is prime. Then cross out any number divisible by 3, etc. This way you can get an arbitrarily large fragment of a sequence of prime numbers. During the time of Eratosthenes, they wrote on wax tablets. The numbers were not crossed out, but punctured. Hence the name of the method – sieve. He designed a device, the mesolabium, for the mechanical solution of the Delian problem (doubling the cube).

Made the first measurement of the size of the earth. Having measured the length of 1/50 of the arc of the earth's meridian, Eratosthenes calculated the circumference of the globe and obtained 25,200 stadia, or 39,960 km, which is only 319 km less than the actual value.

Heron of Alexandria was the great physicist, mathematician, mechanic, and engineer of ancient Greece. He probably lived in the 1st-2nd centuries BC in Alexandria, Egypt. The time of life is attributed to the second half of the first century AD. e. because he gives as an example the lunar eclipse of March 13, 62 AD. e.

Heron is considered one of the greatest engineers in the history of mankind. He was the first to invent automatic doors, an automatic puppet theater, a vending machine, a rapid-fire self-loading crossbow, a steam turbine, automatic decorations, a device for measuring the length of roads (an ancient "taximeter"), etc. He was the first to create programmable devices (a shaft with pins wound on him with a rope).

One of the main services of Heron of Alexandria to history is the books he wrote. They describe not only Heron's inventions but also the knowledge of other scientists of ancient Greece. Many works of Heron of Alexandria were devoted to Mathematics. Most of his works contain formulas on geometry and problems in calculating geometric figures. The famous Heron formula is also described here, with which you can calculate the area of a triangle based on three sides.

At the end of the 2nd century. AD The decline of Greek mathematics begins.

Medical Knowledge and Hippocrates' Contributions

It is difficult to find a person who made such a significant contribution to the development of European medicine as Hippocrates II the Great (c. 460 - c. 377 BC). The reformer of ancient medicine lived in the "golden age" of Pericles - the era of great philosophers, historical writers, poets, playwrights, and sculptors, when Hellenic culture reached its peak. His contemporaries were Socrates, Democritus, Plato, Sophocles, Euripides, Phidias, and Polykleitos. It is no coincidence that it was in Greece that advanced medical thought developed (Hippocrates, Euryphon, Praxagoras, Herophilus, Erasistratus).

Hippocrates (Greek - horse tamer) was born on the island of Kos, located in the south-eastern part of the Aegean Sea, and belonged to the family of the Asclepiads - a corporation of doctors who claimed to be descended from Asclepius, the great physician of Homeric times, recognized as the god of medicine and belonged to the 17th generation of doctors of the Kos school. His teachers were his grandfather Hippocrates I and his father Heraclides, his mother Phenareta (midwife) shared his experience, and in turn, according to tradition, he passed on knowledge to his sons Draco, Thesallus, and son-in-law Polybus. Subsequently, becoming a traveling doctor (periodontist), he traveled a lot and visited Northern and Central Greece, the coast of the Sea of Marmara, and Asia Minor. He continued to study medicine, communicating with local doctors and using votive "tables" that were hung on the walls of the temples of Aesculapius, where cases of healing were recorded. Even during his lifetime, his fame and authority were enormous. The dialogue "Phaedrus" by Plato speaks of the deep philosophical knowledge of Hippocrates. The life of the great healer was long (according to some sources, more than 100 years), and his last refuge was the city of Larissa (Thessaly).

From time immemorial, healing in Ancient Greece was secular; religious ideas did not have such an influence on spiritual life as among the peoples of the East. Medicine was based on empiricism, was free from theurgy (calls to the gods, spells, magical techniques), and developed independently, but there was a connection between it and philosophy. Pythagoras, Alcmaeon, Empedocles, Democritus, Ikkos, Akron and other philosophers (among them were doctors) who studied nature considered the explanation of life processes to be one of the most important problems; they carried out animal dissections and primitive experiments. Hippocrates separated medicine from philosophy, freed it from false theories that dominated observation and experience, and determined the paths for its further development. The means of solving this historical problem was the "Hippocratic method" - observation at the patient's bedside, illumination of experience with the mind, and testing of theory by practice.

In the Mediterranean in the 6th-4th centuries BC. There were several medical schools: Croton (southern Italy), Cyrene (north Africa),

Rhodian (the island of Rhodes), and the most authoritative - Knidos (Asia Minor city of Knidos) and Kos, the recognized head of which was Hippocrates. The Knidos school paid attention mainly to the disease, trying to bring it under one of the many headings and schematizing the treatment. The focus of the Kos school was the patient.

Hippocrates anticipated the view of the dual nature of the disease - the presence in its course of a harmful beginning (pathos) and a beneficial one (sanos), aimed at restoring impaired health. Hippocrates believed that every person has an innate force - "physis" (nature), which under normal conditions regulates all functions of the body. Hippocrates saw the doctor's task as studying the external environment, living conditions, and the patient's surroundings, and stimulating the "physis"; he warned against violent interference in the "natural" course of the disease, calling "first of all, not to harm." This meant that each sick person needed an individual approach: diet, medications, doses, regimen, duration of treatment, everything had to be special, and specific. Thus, Hippocrates established a principle that has been established forever - "to treat not the disease, but the patient."

The logical conclusion of Hippocrates' medical views is a treatment system based on the principles: 1) to benefit and not harm the patient (non nocere); 2) treat the opposite with the opposite (contraria contrariis curantur); 3) coordinate the doctor's actions with nature (Medicus curat, natura sanat); 4) use more active means only when less active ones are not effective.

Hippocrates raised the art of healing to a height that was unknown in Ancient Greece, brought into the system medical knowledge, created the doctrine of etiology, symptoms, diagnosis, stages of the course of diseases, and prediction of ailments, and laid the foundation for the tradition of keeping medical history. His works represent almost all sections of clinical medicine and contain the main core of modern medical terminology (pneumonia, pleurisy, apoplexy, hepatitis, nephritis, diarrhea, dysentery, tetanus, epilepsy, ophthalmia, polytene, paraplegia, etc.).

The name of Hippocrates is associated with the idea of high moral character and ethical behavior of a doctor. He formulated the basic principles of medical deontology and the qualities necessary for a doctor: determination, hard work, constant improvement in his profession, self-esteem, seriousness, friendliness, restraint, aversion to vice, honesty, neatness, the ability to win the trust of the patient, non-covetousness, the ability to store medical confidentiality, putting the interests of the patient above one's self. Hippocrates is credited with the text of the code of ethics ("The Physician's Oath"), which for many centuries has been the basis of the professional obligations of physicians in many countries around the world. He was the first to formulate the eternal principles of medical art: the main goal is the practical treatment of the patient; experience is the true teacher of a doctor; The art of healing can only be learned at the patient's bedside.

Unfortunately, not a single manuscript is known that belonged to Hippocrates. Ancient Greek medical texts in the 3rd century BC. combined into one collection, translated into Latin, it is known as "Corpus Hippocraticum". Some of the works in the collection are attributed to Hippocrates' teachers, his relatives, and students. Although not all of the writings are genuine creations of Hippocrates himself, in general, they fairly fully reflect the main views and methods of treatment established by him and his school. In some of them, the stamp of genius is so clearly visible ("Aphorisms", "Epidemics", "Prognosis", "On Airs, Waters, and Localities") that there can hardly be any doubt as to their affiliation. Eponyms that are mentioned in the collection: "Hippocrates' oath", "the sound of Hippocrates' splashing", "Hippocrates' face", "Hippocrates' fingers", "Hippocrates' cap", "Hippocrates' bench", most likely a tribute to the memory of the most famous doctor of that era. This in no way detracts from his merits, because Hippocrates is the personification of Greek medicine of the classical period, a beautiful and noble legend of Ancient Hellas.

Over 2,500 years, the importance of Hippocrates has been assessed in different ways. Until the early Middle Ages, Hippocrates was well known. In the Middle Ages, Hippocrates, except Byzantium, was almost forgotten, and only in the 16th century did a printed edition of his works appear in Latin by Phoebus Calva with the financial assistance of the great Raphael. "Aphorisms" of Hippocrates were translated into Russian in 1817 by Professor M.Ya. Mudrov. Pearls of medical wisdom are found in abundance in the writings of Hippocrates; in each of his aphorisms and statements, one can feel a brilliant observer and an experienced doctor.

7

Education and Rhetoric

The German philosopher Georg Hegel, being the rector of a classical gymnasium in Nuremberg, was more than once forced to speak to the parents of his students, defending the advantages of ancient Greek education: "And now the noblest nourishing material in the noblest form - golden apples in silver bowls - is contained in the works of the ancients and incomparably more than in any other works of any time or nation. It is enough for me to remind only of the greatness of their way of thinking, of their plastic virtue and love of the fatherland, free from any moral ambiguity, of the greatness of their deeds and characters, of the diversity of their destinies, customs, and disposition of spirit, to justify the statement that in no way The material of education has not been combined with so much that is excellent, amazing, original, versatile and instructive."

Education System In Ancient Greece

In Ancient Greece and the Hellenistic states in the 2nd century BC e. A special three-stage education system developed - this structure existed until the very end of antiquity. The first educational stage is learning to write, read, and count; the second stage - is grammar school. A mandatory element of training here was reading classical writers (poets, orators, historians) with explanations from all fields of knowledge. By the age of 16, schooling ended and third-level education began—the rhetoric school. The main goal of this stage of training was the practical mastery of the art of written and spoken word, that is, oratory. Elements of law (as preparation for a career as a judicial speaker) and philosophy (logic and ethics) were also studied. With the higher humanitarian education of the rhetoric school, specially higher education in the philosophical school coexisted and competed, which claimed the status of an alternative source of knowledge.

In Ancient Greece, several factors emerged that determined the development of pedagogy and education, as well as the philosophy of rationalism, which gradually acquired the status of a special type of knowledge. Firstly, these are specific natural conditions, under the influence of which commerce and handicraft production develop rapidly, which in turn requires certain skills, knowledge, and, of course, the level of education. This predetermined the development of the ancient Greek system of education and schools, where teachers represented a special social class necessary for the training of professional artisans and traders. The classes of traders and artisans represented a serious economic and political force in Ancient Greece, which developed and gained authority in society.

The democratic basis of social organization, which was implemented in the institution of the polis, created conditions for creative freedom and individual initiative and also had a significant impact on ancient Greek education. The third factor that influenced the formation of the educational system in Greece was the development of the philosophy of rationalism, which was generally initiated by reasons of a religious nature. The religious culture of the ancient Greeks was more or less "liberal": the ancient Greek gods were essentially idealized people; the Greeks did not have sacred books (in the sense of divine revelation embodied in the text); did not have a strictly fixed religious and ritual dogma, and the ancient Greek priests did not play a significant role in the life of the polis.

Speaking about the influence of spiritual culture on the formation of the ancient Greek educational model, one cannot fail to mention the role played in this process by the poems of Homer, which became a kind of Bible for the Greeks. Of course, the figure of the singer-storyteller Homer is rather legendary (many researchers consider him to be the same collective character as Shakespeare). However, the ancient Greeks were convinced of the existence of this divinely inspired poet, who single-handedly created large-scale epic canvases that replaced sacred texts. Like the Vedas, intended for the Brahmin priests, or the religious and philosophical texts of the Upanishads, Homer's poems had as their main goal the transfer of sacred knowledge from teacher to student. The tales of the ancient Greeks can also be compared with the Hindu epic poems Ramayana and Mahabharata, which combine stories of mythical and legendary events with adventure plots, love stories, and edifying teachings.

Rhetoric In Ancient Greece

Rhetoric is the science of eloquence. In Greece, since ancient times, beautiful, persuasive, and bright speech has always been valued. They spent decades studying the art of public speaking. These skills were welcomed, and people with the necessary skills were worthy of respect and respect.

It was in ancient Greece that the method of teaching rhetorical principles originated. Ancient thinkers called it "the science of eloquence." Over time, the proximity of Greece to Rome and the constant rivalry between the philosophers of these states led to approximately equal opportunities for both.

What is rhetoric?

From time immemorial, this science has carried within itself the idea of developing a person's logical thinking and his style of expressing thoughts. The main goal is to bring information to people in a form they can understand. Rhetoric acquired importance during the period of mass trials in court and at meetings of elders. The solution to the main state problems could not be achieved without eloquent thinkers, who, through their speeches, brought important facts to the attention of those gathered, giving reasons for every word they said. Rhetorical techniques are still used today by lawyers and prosecutors in their court speeches.

The origin of rhetoric dates back to the 5th century. BC. Hellas became the birthplace of eloquence. Scientists believe that the preconditions for a powerful impetus in the development of this science were laid by the socio-political system of this state. It is known that the cities were ruled by the most revered inhabitants of the people, and the supreme body was the People's Assembly. Politicians and ordinary citizens addressed their questions to the "top" in front of hundreds of people. The trials were also demonstrative. The accused was forced to defend himself, and his life largely depended on the suspect's oratory skills.

Thinkers - the founders of rhetoric

Almost from the first years of the more or less established position of rhetoric and its popularity, teachers of eloquence (sophists) appeared in Greece. For a fee, they gave instructions and trained those wishing to receive rhetoric lessons. The most significant laws of oratory later spread from these masters.

The first textbook of rhetoric was written in the 5th century. BC. Only mentions of that work have reached us. It was created by the Greek Corax, who at one time opened a school of eloquence in Syracuse. It is known that the publication contains the basics of oratory skills.

Later, world-famous philosophers became the authors of their treatises on rhetoric:

1. Socrates.
2. Plato.
3. Cicero.
4. Demosthenes.
5. Pericles.

The experience of Demosthenes is noteworthy. Initially, he spoke so weakly and expressionlessly that the crowd always laughed at his speech. This forced the future unsurpassed speaker to work on himself. He reached such heights in his skill that people listened to him, frozen, and opening their mouths.

Cicero was no less brilliant in his eloquence. He became famous not only for his brilliant skill but also for his work. The treatises saw the light:

1. "Brutus."
2. "About the speaker."
3. "Speaker".

According to the thinker, only a well-educated person could become a speaker. At the same time, he must fight for justice and the happiness of people. The basics of Cicero's works are exercises for optimal rhythm of speech, work on its expressiveness, correct pronunciation, and diction. No less attention was paid to gestures and facial expressions. Speech should become simpler, but at the same time, be sublime and expressive. "The science of convincing through the skill of words," Cicero said about rhetoric.

Rhetoric in Ancient Greece

When the world saw the works of Aristotle, they became relevant. This continued throughout time. They remain so to this day. Aristotle's book was called "Rhetoric". It has 3 parts: general principles (with types of texts for speeches, characteristics, and arguments), names of speakers, and rules for addressing people (the basics of verbal formation of sentences).

The Greek Quintilian produced 12 of his works. The series of books is called "Rhetorical Instructions." The scientist outlined his thoughts on raising a master of oratory, honor, conscience, and successful speech. Attention is also paid to the form of speech presentation. It all starts with an introduction (attack), then the main idea is stated (narration), after which the idea is proven (proof) and a conclusion is drawn (conclusion). In the process, the author's reasoning and conclusions may be inserted into the speech. According to Quintilian, the speaker should "catch" the crowd with his speech, causing people to laugh or get angry. His speech should be clear, correct, and decorated with all kinds of turns, with correct pronunciation.

In general, the ancient Greek philosophers became the founders of the following principles of rhetoric, which became axioms for many years and reached their contemporaries:

1. The basis of eloquence can be a person's natural abilities that need to be developed.
2. The right to speak is given by education and experience as a speaker. An unscientific person cannot convey his ideas to people. The speaker must take into account all the nuances of the topic he is talking about.
3. Speeches are classified. Among them are military, judicial, business, and educational.
4. The basis of eloquence is logical thought, morality, and speech.
5. The science of eloquence is divided into several parts. Among them: working on the content of speech, memorizing it and pronouncing it correctly, and taking advantage of opportunities to win people over.

Over time, the coming era of Christianity completely rejected the ideas of the ancient Greeks as pagans. But from rhetoric, the art of eloquence was adopted for successful church services. The basics of oratory were taught in theological seminaries so that priests could prepare to communicate with people, conveying to them the basic laws of God. The art of oratory also helped in sermons.

The skill of speech is valued no less today than in the days of ancient Greece. The principles of oratory help modern Greeks reach the heights of excellence in their craft and preserve the cultural traditions of the country.

8

Theatre and Performance

Theater (from the Greek "place for spectacle") is an art form that shows the life of society through dramatic action during the performance of actors in front of an audience. It is difficult to imagine modern culture without theater. He has firmly entered our lives and has many fans around the world.

History of the theater

Modern theater has its origins in Ancient Greece. In the 6th century BC. In honor of the god of the harvest and winemaking, Dionysus, festivals were held in Athens - Dionysia. They were accompanied by processions of mummers with loud music. A goat was sacrificed to the deity, while a choir of people dressed as satyrs sang songs. This is where the concept of tragedy comes from - in Greek "song of the goats". During the festivities, noisy, wine-drinking groups of Greeks walked to the altar of Dionysus, which gave the name to the comedy, from the Greek "komos" - a cheerful procession and "odos" - a song. During the Dionysius, plays were staged in Greece and competitions for actors and poets were held.

In 534 BC. playwright Thespis added a one-man performance to the chorus. He read the prologue, which tells the myth of the god Dionysus. Later Heryl and Phrenichus added dialogues between the chorus and the actor, and Aeschylus and Sophocles increased the number of actors to three. This is how the development of the action became possible. They began to create sets for performances and dress the actors in costumes and masks.

The plays were based on alternating speech and choral parts. The prologue began the tragedy and introduced the audience to the characters, the scene of action, and previous events. Then the opening song of the choir (parod) sounded. Next came an alternation of performances by the actors and the choir. In the tragedy, there was always a kommos - a joint part of the actor and the choir- to convey emotional tension. The play ended with an exodus - the departure of the choir and actors from the stage.

One day, three tragedies were shown, united by a common plot. As a rule, these were mythological events, but they revealed the problems of Greek society. In comedies, funny everyday situations were played out, often a satire on famous people and political figures.

The tragedies of Sophocles, Euripides, Aeschylus, and the comedies of Aristophanes and Menander are considered to be the heyday of ancient Greek theatrical art. Ancient plays are staged in modern theaters and have not lost their relevance.

Theatrical Action in Ancient Greece

The theater was very popular in Ancient Greece. The organization of theatrical performances was carried out by one of the city magistrates (archon). He appointed a wealthy citizen who had to pay the costs of the choir, costumes, and decorations - this was considered honorable and increased the sponsor's popularity among the people. The most famous was the theater built in Athens. It accommodated about 17 thousand spectators.

Theatrical performances took place three times a year, during the Dionysius celebration. These were competitions for playwrights who had to present 4 plays: 3 tragedies and 1 satirical drama. In the evening they performed comedies. The competition lasted 3 days, and at the end, the winners were chosen.

At first, admission to the performances was free for everyone, but later a fee of 2 obols was introduced. Since the time of Pericles, a special item of expenditure for spectacles has appeared in the treasury, from which admission to the poor was paid.

People went to the performances with their families, stocking up on food for the whole day. We came to the theater early to take the best seats and chat with our neighbors. Married women were not allowed to attend comedies.

Acting and costumes

Any citizen could become an actor in Ancient Greece. This was considered honorable. There were only 3 actors in a Greek play, so they often had to play multiple roles, changing clothes during the performance.

The actor had to sing and recite well, as well as dance and gesture. Women's roles were played by men. The actors wore masks depicting various characters. The masks were made from wood or fabric soaked in plaster. The mask was worn entirely on the head along with the hair and beard. The masks expressed different emotions: fear, sorrow, fun, anger. If the actor was portraying a real person, the mask was made to resemble his face, but in a grotesque form. Thus, in Aristophanes' comedy "Clouds" a mask was used to depict Socrates. The hole in the mouth and the protrusion on the forehead served as resonators and helped make the voice louder. During one performance, the actor could change different masks. Women's masks were white, and men's were dark. They also differed in the age and social status of the characters. There were masks depicting men and women of different ages, slaves, gods, mythical creatures, forces of nature, and abstract concepts (envy, death, madness, guilt, etc.).

To be visible from afar, the actors wore high-soled shoes - buskins. Overlays were worn under clothing to create volume in certain areas for comic or tragic effects. The costume also mattered. The actors wore a chiton with long sleeves that went down to the floor, and cloaks - long or short. Comedian actors had short chitons. Kings wore purple cloaks, queens wore white cloaks with a purple border. The clothes of the exiles were dirty white; black was considered the color of misfortune. Unlucky people wore blue or green cloaks, and happy people wore yellow or red ones. Gods or heroes appeared with their recognizable attributes: Apollo with a bow and arrows, Hercules with a club and a lion's skin, old men with a staff, kings with a staff, etc.

Architecture of Ancient Greek Theater

Orchestra

In Ancient Greece, the theater was located in an open space. It consisted of a round platform (orchestra) and spectator seats located in a semicircle on the hillside.

Initially, the orchestra was a place where sacrifices were made to Dionysus. It first appeared on the slopes of the Acropolis in Athens. They danced and sang praises on it in honor of Dionysus. In the center of the orchestra stood an altar. On its steps, a flutist-aulet played or an actor-protagonist stood answering the choir. The altar remained in its place later, when there was no longer any talk about the cult of Dionysus, as a tribute to tradition.

Seats for spectators - theater

At first, people just sat on the hillsides. Later, seats were built for them: wooden, then stone. They were located in a semicircle around the orchestra. Below there were places for the nobility, honorary citizens, and priests. They could have stone backs and canopies for comfort. Above were places for the "middle class" and at the top for the poor. Longitudinal passages (parods) divided places into sectors and upper and lower places.

Scan

In the 5th century BC, a scene appears behind the orchestra. Originally this was a tent for changing clothes for actors. Later, the scene is an architectural structure adjacent to the orchestra and depicts a temple or palace. It is a stage backdrop. Proskenia are attached to the sides of the scene to improve acoustics. They stored acting props and were also used as decorations. The Greeks used painted sets and mechanical machines in their plays. The entire theater was built in such a way that it maintained excellent audibility so that people in the highest places could hear the actors' lines.

Ancient Greek theater was a unique phenomenon that had a huge impact on world culture. The basic principles of ancient theater are still used in dramaturgy. Then in our time, the theater served as a kind of mirror in which society could see its problems and shortcomings.

III

Legacy and Influence

9

Greek Culture in the Modern World

Many of the great achievements of Ancient Greece influence today's European culture. To this day, we draw on the following tools bequeathed to us by the Greeks - Democracy, Science, Philosophy, Art, Architecture, Olympic Games.

Democracy

Democracy (demos – people, Kratos – force) – the power of the people. It had its origins in ancient Athens. By the 5th century BC, Athens had abandoned the monarchy system and moved to full democracy. Initially, the aristocracy began to take power. Over time, officials began to be elected in the people's assembly by all citizens. People's assemblies were supposed to give ordinary citizens influence on the affairs of the polis, but ultimately they had a strictly informational character. This led to deepening differences between social classes, which resulted in increased social dissatisfaction. This dissatisfaction influenced changes in Athenian society.

It was ordered that customary laws be written down and the order

107

of policies be regulated. One of the Athenian archons, Drakon, was appointed for this purpose in 621 BC. The laws written by him were very strict, so they did not have a positive impact on improving the life of Athenian society. At the same time, it should be emphasized that the laws written by Drakon constitute the first code of criminal and civil law.

The aristocracy was finally forced to make concessions, and further reforms were carried out, authored by Solon. He was the first archon - the highest state official, today's equivalent of the prime minister. It prepared the ground for political changes in Athens. He divided Athenian society into 4 classes - according to their wealth. He established a new institution - the Council of Four Hundred, which became the most important state body. Additionally, he established a jury court and had the ultimate influence on expanding the powers of the assembly of full-fledged citizens of Athens who were over 20 years old (ecclesia).

Further reforms were carried out in the years 508 - 507 BC by Cleisthenes. These reforms laid the foundations for Athenian democracy. The reforms aimed to limit the role of the aristocracy blur property differences and mix society. He changed the division into brotherhoods, tribes, and families into a territorial division, Attica was divided into 3 districts. Each district was divided into smaller regions. Every foreigner who came to Attica and settled there permanently gained civil rights. He increased the number of councilors from 400 to 500 - 50 citizens from each division, they were elected annually by lot. He established a shell court and the office of 10 chiefs - the result of the administrative division into 10 tribes.

Pericles is considered the father of democracy. During his time, Athens developed economically, socially, and culturally. Additionally, during his time, allowances were introduced for officials, which enabled less wealthy people to take up office.

Science

The development of Greek culture had a huge impact on today's science. The range of sciences that developed in ancient Greece is huge and includes such disciplines as mathematics, astronomy, medicine, geography, and philosophy. The period of development of science in ancient Greece is called by historians the "golden age of science".

During these times, famous theorems were created that are still used in mathematics today - the Pythagorean theorem and the Thales theorem. Additionally, Euclid published the work "The Elements of Geometry", which covered areas such as geometry and number theory. This work was used as a textbook for the next 2,200 years.

Apollonis is the creator of trigonometry and the precursor of analytical geometry. He introduced concepts still used today - ellipse, hyperbola, parabola. Thanks to Thales of Miletus, it was possible to calculate, for example, the height of the pyramids, as well as the distance of the ship from the shore.

The Pythagoreans discovered that the Earth was spherical and revolved around the Sun. They discovered 10 other planets. Eratosthenes measured the radius of the Earth and the length of the equator. Hipparchus estimated the distance from the Earth to the Moon and also created a coordinate grid.

The forerunner of today's medicine was Hippocrates (Hippocratic

Oath) - who put the patient's health as the most important thing. He is the creator of the principle "Primo non nocere" - First, not harm. He described the amputation of limbs and the use of prostheses. He developed a tool for treating scoliosis. He drew attention to the need for hygiene and diets to prevent diseases. He set the basis for the diagnosis. Proxagoros – distinguish between arteries and veins. The duodenum, pancreas, and prostate gland were isolated by Herophilos.

Aristotle made a huge contribution to the development of science. He developed theories of the state and dealt with the history of theater, philosophy, logic, and systematized animals. He founded a school in which teams undertook scientific research and gathered scientists from many fields. In Alexandria - following the example of Aristotle's school - a Museum (Museion) was established, which was a scientific institute. There was a huge library there, with a collection of 700,000 papyrus scrolls (books).

Philosophy

Ancient Greek philosophy had a huge influence on the formation of later sciences. She focused her attention on the role of reason and research. Philosophy comes from the Greek word philosophia, which means love of wisdom. Greek philosophers focused on reality, rejecting the belief that the world around them was obvious.

Thales of Miletus is considered the first philosopher. He created the theory that everything was created and composed of water. He based his theory on observations and reducing nature (nature, the divine world) to one basic principle.

The classical Greek philosopher was Socrates, considered the founder of Western philosophy. He contributed to ethics, logic, and the theory of knowledge.

Plato wrote dozens of philosophical dialogues. They affected the methods of acquiring knowledge (early dialogues), the justice system, and practical ethics. In his works, he assessed metaphysics, reason, ethics, and knowledge. He is assessed as a rationalist and idealist.

Aristotle's most famous treatises are "Physics", "Metaphysics", "Nicomachean" (Ethics), "De anima" (On the Soul), "Politics. Aristotle was a philosopher and thinker. His views dominated for over 2,000 years.

Art

The three most important historical periods that best reflect the essence of Greek art: are archaic (700 - 480 BC), classical (480 - 323 BC), and Hellenistic (323 - 31 BC).

Greek sculptures are the best preserved to this day. In the classical period, sculptures perfectly reflected the shape of the human body, as well as gestures and muscle play. An example is Myron's "Discobolus", where the artist showed the body before throwing the disc under maximum tension.

Polycletus of Argos is considered the master of static sculpture, his most famous work is Doryphoros (from Greek "doryphoros", meaning spearbearer). Polyclitus sought to recreate the beauty that existed in nature. For this purpose, he made numerous measurements from which he derived ideal values. He achieved such perfection that he could create a work of art based only on the thickness of the finger or the length of the foot.

Lysippos made sculpture three-dimensional. He introduced illusionism - he made the head smaller and the body slimmer to make it seem taller. Lusipp's most famous work is Apoxyomenos - an athlete cleansing himself of sand.

Architecture

The Acropolis, whose reconstruction took about 40 years, is an example of wonderful Greek architecture. The sculptor Phidias was the author of the plan to rebuild the Acropolis. The culmination of the first phase of architectural development was the Temples of the Acropolis. This complex of buildings had a huge impact on subsequent eras, which added little to each other.

Then it was time for utility buildings. A portico, a characteristic type of public building, is an elongated hall in which one of the walls is replaced by a colonnade, and the other is a wall or a series of rooms.

The place of official meetings was the Greek Theater. There were theaters in every city and performances were performed there. Theaters were usually located on the hillsides outside the city.

Olympic Games

The Olympic Games were the most prestigious sporting event in ancient Greece, held in honor of Zeus. They were held only in summer, every four years. Only men were allowed in the audience and participants.

The participant had to be physically fit. The disciplines were individual, there were no group disciplines. The games were always held in the same place - Olympia in the Peloponnese. These were pan-Greek competitions intended to remind citizens that despite the ongoing fighting, they were still one nation. Additionally, during the games, all battles were suspended, a truce was concluded, and God's peace reigned - Ekecheria.

Modern games also aim to spread the idea of peace. In ancient times (as well as today), the opening and closing of the games were a spectacular event. Another common feature is the Olympic flame, which was present in ancient times and today.

10

Rediscovering Greek Knowledge

A common thesis is that many ancient Greek texts may have been lost if not for the preservation efforts of Islamic scholars, and while this may be true to some extent, it was ultimately the Byzantine Empire that ensured the continued existence of ancient Greek ideas.

Meeting the Arab World with Ancient Greek Knowledge

Arab and Islamic scholars' introduction to ancient Greek philosophy, science, medicine, and technology occurred during the Umayyad invasion and subsequent conquest of previously Hellenized territories in Egypt and the Levant around the 7th century.

Arab logicians and thinkers preserved ancient Greek knowledge on which Islamic art, architecture, literature, philosophy, and technological advances were based. Ibn Khaldun, an Arab historian, wrote: "The sciences of only one people, the Greeks, have reached us because they were translated through the efforts of Caliph Al-Mavun. He was successful in this direction because he had many translators at his disposal and he spent a lot of money on it."

However, from the very beginning, many Arabs were against classical learning, and because of this, the religious caliphs could not support scientific translations of ancient Greek works. Instead, translators had to seek wealthy—rather than religious—patrons for their work.

Translations and commentaries by Islamic scholars on ancient Greek texts gradually made their way through the Arab-conquered parts of the West into Spain and Sicily, which became important centers for the transmission of ideas.

However, a significant amount of translation was carried out only during the reign of the Abbasids, which followed the rule of the Umayyads, in the 8th century. Much of the knowledge of the Greek language during Umayyad rule was acquired from the Greek language scholars who still existed from the Byzantine period, rather than through large-scale translation and dissemination of texts.

Most of the transfers took place during the Abbasid period, when the second Abbasid caliph Al-Mansur moved the capital from Damascus to Baghdad. It was here that he founded the House of Wisdom, a huge library containing Greek classical texts.

Al-Mansur ordered the translation of these texts into Arabic, and under him, translations were made from Greek, Syriac, and Persian. The last two were themselves translations from Greek or Sanskrit.

The 6th-century king of Persia, Anushirvan the Just, also introduced several ancient Greek ideas into his kingdom.

Ancient Greek knowledge preserved by the Byzantines was then passed on to Islamic scholars

However, the ancient Greek texts and culture that we value today ultimately would not have been preserved if not for the efforts of the scholars and monks of the Byzantine period. It was they who, at various times throughout history, passed on this knowledge to the rest of Europe and the Islamic world.

Aristotle was translated in France at the Abbey of Mont Saint-Michel before the translations of the great Greek philosopher into Arabic. Arabic translations came through Syriac by Christian scholars from the conquered lands of the Byzantine Empire.

The most famous works of the classical era, especially Greek, were easily accessible to the Byzantines and Western peoples who had cultural and diplomatic ties with the Byzantine Empire. Of the Greek classics in existence today, at least 75 percent are known from Byzantine copies, according to Michael Harris's book A History of Libraries in the Western World.

Another historian, John Julius Norwich, argued that "much of what we know about antiquity, especially about Hellenic and Roman literature and Roman law, would have been lost forever if not for the scholars and scribes of Constantinople."

Similarly, Ibn Khaldun also reported that the Abbasid caliph Al-Mansur requested the mathematical works of the Greeks from the Byzantine emperor.

11

Alexander the Great and the Spread of Hellenistic Culture

chaemenid state in the 4th century BC was heading towards decline. The breakdown of the state system became more and more apparent, and significant territories were lost. In 336 BC. On the Persian throne was a representative of the sideline of the Achaemenids, who took the throne name Darius III. Several years of his reign marked the time of the collapse of the Achaemenid power 1.

Development of Greek city-states at the turn of the 5th - 4th centuries. led to a socio-political and economic crisis. The introduction of slavery undermined the unity of the civil collective and led to property and social differentiation. Within the framework of the policies, the relationship between the rich and the poor, the demos and the aristocracy became aggravated. More and more often, claims were made by one or another of the states that were strengthening from time to time for hegemony in Hellas, for the creation of a union of Greek cities.

In the political struggle, different policies (most often Athens) were in the lead, but gradually the center of gravity began to move north, to Macedonia. The political system of Macedonia differed from the Greek policies: it was a hereditary monarchy, somewhat limited by a meeting of warriors and a council of nobility. All the land belonged to the monarch, and he gave it for use, demanding military service for this. The land was cultivated not by slaves, but by free people.

The weakening of polis Greece coincided with the strengthening of the political power of Macedonia. Its king, Philip II, an intelligent and energetic ruler, not only reorganized and strengthened the army but also began to actively intervene in the internecine wars of the policies. He subjugated most of the policies of Hellas and began to prepare for a campaign in the East, against the Achaemenids. However, amid military preparations in 336, Philip died as a result of a conspiracy. The Macedonian throne passed to his son, 20-year-old Alexander.

Hellenistic era in the Middle East

Conquests of Alexander the Great

From the age of 16, Philip II began to involve his son in state affairs: having gone on a campaign against Byzantium, he left Alexander to rule the state, and in the Battle of Chaeronea the young man commanded the cavalry.

Having come to power, Alexander brutally dealt with the murderers of his father and possible contenders for the throne. Within about a year, the young king destroyed internal opposition, pacified the northern tribes, and brought the Greeks to submission. Nothing else stood in the way of the long-awaited campaign in the spring of 334 BC. Alexander crossed the Hellespont (Dardanelles) and set foot on Asian soil.

Alexander's army did not know defeat. By 324 BC. Significant territories came under the rule of Alexander and a huge, hitherto unprecedented empire arose, which included Macedonia, most of the policies of Balkan and island Greece, regions of the former Persian state, and part of North-West India.

Orders in the conquered territory

By force of arms, Alexander united a variety of countries and peoples - the cultural Greek city-states and Macedonia, which still retained the remnants of the primitive communal system, the Nile Valley, and Mesopotamia with their thousand-year-old culture, the nomadic tribes of eastern Iran. This power did not have a single economic base and was a purely military association.

During the campaign, conquest came down mainly to the capture of cities, strategically important strongholds, and roads, and the establishment of general control - military, administrative, and financial. Moving along the coast, Alexander expelled the oligarchs from everywhere and established a democratic system, the cities were granted freedom and autonomy. This policy was largely determined by tactical considerations: the old rulers usually relied on the oligarchs, thereby making the democrats natural supporters of Alexander. However, the freedom that was granted to the policies remained largely purely nominal, because the cities came under the authority of Alexander, who autocratically interfered in their internal affairs.

In addition, to pursuing military goals, Alexander founded new cities, seeing in them the strongholds of his power. Therefore, they were built where population resistance was especially strong. Such cities were not polises with their self-government bodies; the composition of their population was mixed. These were the king's subjects, placed under the control of his representatives.

The foundations of the new management system were reliance on local nobility, separation of administrative, financial, and military management, streamlining of tax collection and coinage, and respect for local customs and gods.

Alexander limited himself to recognizing his power and paying taxes. In living conditions, especially in areas remote from the center, no radical change occurred.

Alexander's power was maintained by military force and needed to be strengthened. Alexander made Babylon the center of his multinational power. To strengthen the unity of the state and smooth out the contradictions between the conquerors and the vanquished, Alexander pursued a policy of "merging peoples" 1. A striking example of this policy was the wedding in Susa when 10 thousand soldiers - Greeks and Macedonians - married local girls. Alexander himself married Darius's eldest daughter. All newlyweds received a rich dowry. This idea, according to A.I. Nemirovsky, "did not have any results, but gave another reason to accuse him [Alexander] of despotism and departure from the Greek-Macedonian religious and everyday traditions." Such activity rather indicates a desire to expand the social base, to create a kind of "dominant people", a faithful support of power, and "an instrument of oppression and exploitation of other peoples" 2. By uniting the Macedonians with the Persians, Alexander thereby reduced them to the level of subjects.

Alexander carried out reforms in the army. He ordered that soldiers "unfit for military service due to old age and injuries" be sent home. In their places, he recruited 30 thousand local youths, trained in Greek literacy and handling of Macedonian weapons.

Another of Alexander's activities is the forced deification of his personality. Perhaps the idea of using his deification for political purposes as a means of strengthening power arose with Alexander back in Egypt, where the priests declared him the son of Amun. In any case, attributing divine origin to himself went in the general vein of his policy and was supposed to sanctify his power.

All these events caused dissatisfaction among the army and increased social tension.

The essence of Hellenism

During Alexander's campaign and after it, a large stream of Greeks and Macedonians poured into the East, and settled here, bringing other forms of social relations. Some of the cities built by Alexander became centers of political and economic life. As a result of the campaign, the geographical boundaries of the then-world expanded, new communication routes were laid, and shipping expanded - all this contributed to the development of the economy and trade relations. The hike brought new knowledge in the fields of geography, biology, and ethnography. It marked the beginning of a new stage in the history of the Eastern Mediterranean, which is characterized by complex and contradictory processes of interaction between Greco-Macedonian and local principles - the Hellenistic era.

After the death of Alexander, the collapse of the world power and the creation of new states began. The closest generals of Alexander the Great (Diodochi) shared the inheritance of their late ruler for more than 40 years. The idea of a single empire was very popular: the rulers of individual regions were considered as satraps of one entity. However, the Philip-Alexander dynasty was interrupted, and not one of the diadochi had sufficient strength or moral right to claim the role of supreme ruler of the entire empire. Now each diadokh thought about consolidating power for himself and his descendants in one or another part of the state.

By the beginning of the 3rd century. BC. The place of a single power was taken by several independent states in which power was concentrated in the hands of the Greco-Macedonian conquerors. These states, according to the definition of the German historian of the 19th century. Johann Droysen was called "Hellenistic" 1.

Hellenism is the forced unification of the ancient Greek and ancient Eastern worlds, which previously developed separately, into a single system of states. As a result, a unique society and culture was created, which differed both from the Greek proper and from the ancient Eastern social structure and culture itself. It was a synthesis of ancient Greek and ancient Eastern civilizations, which gave a qualitatively new socio-economic structure, political superstructure, and culture.

Both ancient Greek and ancient Eastern societies were declining. The Greek polis, ensured the economic rise of Greece, the creation of a dynamic social structure, a mature republican structure, including various forms of democracy, and the creation of a remarkable culture, by the middle of the 4th century. BC. exhausted its internal capabilities and became a brake on historical progress. Against the backdrop of constant tension between classes, an acute social struggle unfolded between the oligarchy and the democratic circles of citizenship, which led to tyranny and self-destruction. Coalitions of individual city-states constantly fought among themselves, sometimes uniting, breaking up.

The ancient Eastern world, was united with the Persian Empire, in the middle of the 4th century. BC was also experiencing a serious socio-political crisis. Its conservative, sedentary social structure was at the stage of decay. The stagnant economy did not allow the development of vast expanses of empty land. No new cities were built. Little attention was paid to trade; huge reserves of currency metal lay in treasuries and were not put into circulation. Traditional communal structures were disintegrating, and the process of spreading private farms as more dynamic production units was slow and painful. Ties between the central government and local rulers weakened, and separatism of individual parts became commonplace.

If Greece suffered from excessive activity in internal political life, overpopulation, and limited resources, it historically needed to unite within the framework of a large state entity with a strong central government that would ensure internal order, external security, and the possibility of further development, then the Persian monarchy, on the contrary, suffered failures due to stagnation, weak use of potential opportunities, disintegration of individual parts. These different socio-economic and political systems could ideally complement each other. This synthesis became the Hellenistic societies and states formed after the collapse of the world power of Alexander the Great.

Hellenism became a new, more progressive stage in the development of ancient Greek and ancient Eastern societies. The outflow of a significant part of the population of Hellas to the East relieved for some time the acute social situation in Greek cities and contributed to overcoming crisis phenomena in the policies.

The formation of a greater territorial unity, and the establishment of close ties between different parts of the Hellenistic world, expanded the possibilities of the Hellenistic economy as a whole, including Hellas, Macedonia, Magna Graecia, and the Black Sea region. In these regions, economic, ethnic, and cultural contacts with the surrounding local tribes (Thracians, Scythians, Sarmatians) intensified, an increase in unification tendencies was observed, and stronger city federations than in classical times emerged (Achaean, Aetolian unions) or state formations of a new type, which included, in addition to the Greek city-states, local tribes (Sicilian state, Bosporus).

Colonization on an unprecedented scale led to the emergence of dozens of new cities, similar to classical Greek city-states, i.e. being self-governing territories. These policies had autonomous forms of administration, as well as privileges and immunities. True, there could be no talk of their political independence: all urban settlements that arose according to the Hellenistic type were included in a unified system of state administration, and the kings invariably sought to bring the cities under their control. The rights of land ownership in these cities were enjoyed not only by full citizens but also by other settlers, which dramatically changed the nature of the status of the city's civil community. Through such settlements, elements of Greek culture, the social and political system, the economy, and the way of life of the Greeks penetrated the Middle East region. The most important in this regard was the new capital of Egypt, Alexandria.

However, such penetration affected only the most economically and culturally developed areas and segments of the population. As for remote areas or ancient commercial and industrial centers like Babylon, they largely retained their usual structure and borrowed little from the Greeks, except to strengthen ties with them.

Thus, the entire territory of the Middle Eastern region was, as it were, divided into two unequal parts: into Hellenistic and Hellenized cities and settlements, which included in their sphere of influence the court and senior service nobility, part of the administration apparatus, as well as wealthy representatives of the private sector, and into little connected with by these centers the periphery, which continued to live its former life. This periphery became known as the hora.

Achievements of Hellenism

The expansion of the territorial framework of the Hellenistic ecumene and the closer interaction of its various parts had a beneficial effect, first of all, on economic life. This was reflected in the rapid development of trade and commodity-money relations. Old ones were resumed and new trade routes were opened (for example, from Alexandria to India via the Nile, the Red Sea, the Bab el-Mandeb Strait, and the Arabian Sea). The Hellenistic kings took energetic measures to encourage trade operations (protection of trade routes, tax incentives for merchants, construction of roads). The development of trade was accompanied by the massive minting of coins from reserves of precious metal, stored in the form of ingots in the basements of the Persian kings.

An indicator of the active development of the Hellenistic economy was intensive urban planning: in the Hellenistic era, over 170 large and small cities of the Greek type were founded. The newly founded cities became major craft, trade, and cultural centers.

Social-class relations have become noticeably more complicated. In each Hellenistic country, there was a combination of relations of the developed polis type with the traditional communal structure of the ancient Eastern type: along with the class of dependent workers of different statuses, the total number of slaves of the classical type increased. The structure of the ruling class also became more complex: it included not only representatives of the local aristocracy but also foreigners (Greeks, Macedonians) who made up its top. The contradiction between the local and the Greco-Macedonian aristocracy complicated the social struggle as a whole.

A new form of government emerged, replacing the traditional types of sovereign Greek polis and ancient Eastern despotism - the Hellenistic monarchy. It combined, in different variations, elements of both polis statehood and ancient Eastern monarchical orders. The deification of the ruler, his unlimited power, the presence of a permanent bureaucratic apparatus, royal ownership of a significant part of the land, and a professional army (signs of eastern despotism) was combined with the self-government of cities with several privileges, where private ownership of land was recognized, a People's Assembly was assembled, a council and magistrates were elected, Some policy institutions functioned.

The expansion of the ecumene gave a powerful impetus to the development of culture. During the Hellenistic era, the movement and mixing of the population intensified, the mental horizons were enriched, and the creativity of each person intensified. The social structure of Hellenistic society, which involved a combination of polis-type slaveholding and ancient Eastern communal relations, a variety of social and class contradictions, and the instability of the Hellenistic social system as a whole created a special social atmosphere, which was embodied in various ideological systems and manifested itself differently in different spheres of culture.

The state made attempts to direct cultural creativity in the right direction, allocating significant funds to finance certain industries (opening a museum).

The role of religion has increased. The mixing of Greek and Eastern cultures led to the interpenetration of religions, new deities appeared that combined the features of ancient Greek and ancient Eastern deities (Sarapsis). In general, the Hellenistic period was characterized by an active search for new religious forms and ideas. A craving for monotheism began to appear, and interest in the ethical side of religious teachings increased. In religious searches, ideas were born that later became the basis of Christianity.

Such searches reflected the increasing complexity of social and political life, the instability of the situation in the Hellenistic countries, and the changes caused by these processes in the general worldview of people. In the conditions of constant movement of large masses of people across the vast territory of the Hellenistic world, a person's connection with his hometown was interrupted. He began to feel like a citizen of the world, a cosmopolitan. The foundations of collectivism were undermined, a sense of individualism, faith in one's strength, and luck appeared. This had a significant impact on philosophy, which was striking in its diversity of ideas and philosophical schools (Academics, Peripatetics, Stoics, Epicureans, Cynics).

In literature, there was an increase in the number of writing authors, which indicated an increase in the interest of a wide mass of readers in literary works. Hellenistic literature was amazed with its diversity of genres. Attention to form increased, and the ideological content of the works became less profound. Literature was characterized by a high interest in everyday life, increased psychologism, and attention to the inner world of man. The stories became more realistic.